Selling to Informal Markets

A corporate blueprint for successfully
selling to Africa's informal retailers

Selling to Informal Markets

A corporate blueprint for successfully selling to Africa's informal retailers

By Farayi L. Ziswa

Printed in South Africa & Kenya, First Edition, 2025

ISBN 978-1-77928-645-1

Book interior edited by Simbarashe L. Manyeruke

Designed by Makanaka Productions

Cover artwork by McMillan Shemangale

Author's photograph by Tallgrass Media

Connect with the author at coach@inheritege.com

www.inheritege.com

DEDICATION

To my wife, Janet. Thank you for the encouragement and inspiring support.

To my late mum, Mrs. Margaret Ziswa, whose legacy lives on every page. This book is rooted in the lessons she planted in me from my youth.

ACKNOWLEDGEMENTS

Writing this book has been one of the most humbling and rewarding experiences of my life. It is not just a product of research or strategy; it is a reflection of the people, places, and lessons that shaped me.

To the business leaders that invested in BTL Consulting and to the numerous work colleagues that walked the market with me, seeking to increase product visibility and improve the availability of product in the informal markets, thank you.

To the countless retailers across Africa's informal markets—thank you. Over the past 27 years, your grit, wisdom, and generosity have been the driving force behind this work. You welcomed me into your world, shared your stories, and showed me what true enterprise looks like.

To the team leaders and sales teams at BTL Consulting Ltd—past and present—thank you for walking this journey with me. We have had wins, setbacks, and drama, but each moment contributed to our growth and success. Looking back, it was all worthwhile.

Peter van As— your belief in me, your support, and your partnership over the years have meant more than words can say. You invested in me when it mattered the most, and I'll never forget that.

To my mentors, especially John Kachambwa and Duncan Manyonda(ADM)—thank you for speaking into my life. Your wisdom helped shape not just this book, but the man behind it.

PREFACE

The significance of sales and the art of selling in organisations of all sizes cannot be emphasised enough. While extensive literature exists on selling skills and techniques, there is a distinct lack of resources tailored to the indigenous African context, particularly focused on the informal markets.

This book is for retail entrepreneurs, executives in manufacturing and distribution businesses, both professional and aspiring sales professionals, as well as participants in the informal market. They drive Africa's economies, facilitating transactions worth billions of dollars each and every day.

If you sell goods or services within Africa's informal markets and have encountered challenges in persuading customers, explaining your products, or closing sales, this guide provides effective tools to improve your outcomes. It offers practical steps, authentic case studies, and a proven sales framework to succeed in the market.

The guidance herein will enable you to engage confidently with customers, increase your sales efficiency, build trust across markets, and distinguish yourself—even in highly competitive environments. This manual is grounded in practical experience rather than theory and serves as a firsthand resource for those conducting bona fide business.

Whether you aim to expand your business or enhance your team's capabilities, this blueprint is designed for you. Thank you for choosing this book. May it support your professional growth, sharpen your skills, make you a better leader, inspire those around you and, most importantly, grow your sales.

TABLE OF CONTENTS

INTRODUCTION

I was raised in Harare, Zimbabwe, and often visited my parents' commercial farm in Headlands, a three-hour drive away from the bustling capital city. At the farm, we grew tobacco and maize and did some horticulture for export.

By the time I was thirteen, I was already doing several administrative tasks on the farm, and one of my duties was managing the payroll.

Together with my cousins, we would, monthly, calculate the wages and pay the workers individually in cash. To provide a sense of security, given we were dealing with people twice our age and size, Rover, a rottweiler, was always by my side, ready to handle any threat.

After paying the workers, we would rush to the farm store (that we would have replenished the day before) to serve clients and restock the shelves now and again. We made sure that our sales brought in some profit.

Come nighttime, we jumped over to the bottle store, which was always abuzz with revellers, especially during month ends. To keep the people entertained, a local band played. I remember watching them strum their guitars and play tin drums that were connected to a tractor battery-operated amplifier. Some of those parties would go on until the next morning, and all the while we would be behind the counter, manning the tills and replenishing stock.

On mid-month weekends, my mother would take us to her shop in Marondera, Zimbabwe, 60 km away from Harare, and we would spend the day serving customers, running the cash till and restocking the shelves. By the end of the day, utterly exhausted, we would bundle ourselves into the red VW Golf, drive back home and arrive late at night.

Just after turning sixteen, I got my driving licence, and it was such a relief for my mother, as I could now independently do most of the errands.

All the businesses I have talked about still exist today, albeit under different management.

As I helped my parents on the farm and in their businesses, I did not realise at that time that I was getting soaked into the world of informal markets and enjoying it. During those early years of my life, I learnt to keep a close eye on competition and pricing, working with wholesalers and gained so many insights that I will share in this book.

At nineteen, after finishing high school, I went to the UK for my university education, where I completed a bachelor's degree in business accounting and a master's degree in financial management from Hull University.

To supplement the fees and living costs, I trained to be a nurse and progressed in the industry to do ward and theatre nursing at a prestigious hospital in London, where I specialised in orthopaedics.

As much as that was an awkward diversion in my career, it taught me empathy, time management, patience and attention to detail.

Soon after graduating, I resigned from nursing and started working towards what I anticipated would be a rewarding career in treasury and finance.

I joined a multinational organisation on their two-year management training programme, and that fast-tracked my apprenticeship in manufacturing, cost and financial accounting, human resource management, procurement, marketing and other managerial aspects of international corporate business operations. That training and knowledge I gained became extremely valuable when the time came to establish my own businesses.

After completing the graduate trainee programme, I was promoted to be a manager in Treasury and had a string of impressive debt collection results in a season that was characterised by hyperinflation in the country.

A senior director, who later became my boss, would one day walk into my office with an unexpected proposition. He suggested that my debt collection success was primarily because of my success in relationship management, and he concluded that my true calling was not in finance but in sales. He wanted me to join his sales department.

His offer left me bewildered and a bit ruffled. How could anyone suggest that I transition to a department that, at the time, I had no experience in and that was led by career salespeople who delivered incredible results based on relationships and pure grit!

It did not make sense to leave what I had mastered academically and professionally for a role with seemingly no personal growth potential.

But he was a consummate salesperson and did not give up. Once I had gotten past the initial shock of being invited to join sales, he offered more clarity on why he believed in my potential.

"Corporate selling is all about numbers, and you are a numbers guy," he emphasised. "Sales create the numbers through every transaction. We need to make sure the numbers make sense and make the numbers bring more sales. Who better than you, the accountant, to do this!"

He spoke of a new revolution in sales, one that would be driven by statistically tracking and analysing customers, transactions, product movement, shelf visibility and more. Numbers, numbers, numbers, equalling structured analytical growth—that was his pitch.

I knew the business was looking to restructure its sales division and move away from impulsive trends where the company's profitability was influenced by wholesalers who knew when to bulk order and maximise their discounts, based on our predictable internal desperation to meet sales targets at month-end. The current team was not likely to bring that change, so after some persuasion, I made the awkward decision to move from finance to sales.

I must admit that it was not a walk in the park. I quickly realised there was a lot to learn about sales. It was a gruelling yet incredible learning season. One thing I had to do quickly was learn to leave my desk and embrace the constant travelling and working in the field. I also had to master how to interact with customers and build relationships, which was the exact opposite of my previous desk job. Where in the past I reported sales figures delivered by others, I now had to bring in the sales and have an answer for every product's performance. In addition, I had to get out of my introverted nature and meet clients as well as manage and motivate my team; people whose performance I used to observe and sometimes criticise.

Furthermore, I had to go back to the classroom to learn what were then new concepts in selling: Category Management, Channel Management, Route-to-Market Management and Trade Marketing. I had to train those concepts and implement them for my teams and customers. We successfully developed rollout strategies for our customers across Southern and East Africa and started the programme in modern trade.

Using the new strategies, we tracked our product sales, as well as our availability and visibility in the formal and informal markets. During an era before widespread use of mobile phones, we started the first foray into using mobile tracking systems using PDA units, the initial attempts at online reporting. In addition to learning about the technical aspects of sales, there were many soft skills that I needed to learn, such as dealing with resistance and objections. What a season! What learnings! What fun!

Several projects that we rolled out became case studies within the business and were used for roll-outs across Africa. Instead of being the pushover department, mocked for just winging it by other departments, we now had a specific mandate and our own irrefutable strategies for success.

Twenty-seven years later, most of what we rolled out then is now standard in corporate and retail organisations throughout Africa, whether in the informal or formal markets.

Technology has made substantial contributions to the development of sales practices. The integration of mobile technology, e-commerce, and mobile payment solutions such as MPESA has driven considerable progress across manufacturing, retail management, outlet monitoring, merchandising, retail promotions, and the broader sales sector. As a result, consumers now enjoy a wider selection of products, delivered more frequently and at reduced costs.

After working in various executive commercial roles in the Middle East and African markets, I took the audacious step in 2010 of establishing a sales and selling organisation in Kenya. I had identified a gap in knowledge between large multinational organisations and smaller enterprises in terms of developing and executing their sales strategies when selling to informal markets.

Leading multinational brands were present in informal markets, but competition was negligibly visible. What was common was localised competition. Kiosks stocked what they bought from wholesalers, which was dictated by above-the-line advertisements like billboards, TV and radio advertising. Suppliers that were unable to advertise were excluded by wholesalers and lacked national visibility in informal markets. The biggest loser was the consumer who was denied variety, sometimes quality and the best prices.

Our organisation promised to help small to medium organisations get their footprint in the informal market on a national scale, with maximised availability, visibility and rock-solid performance tracking tools.

Convincing small and medium-sized enterprises to adopt our service was not easy. They often thought we were just another marketing ploy. But it paid off for the early adopters: leading multinational organisations that recognised the opportunity and found it cheaper to roll out through us. Collaborating with us was also a versatile training platform for their internal staff.

Ultimately, the results were in their favour, as their presence (nationally) in informal markets expanded from an average of 30% to over 65% within a few months. With the increase in product range in the kiosks, they also enjoyed an increase in overall cash-driven income, increased retail visibility in-store and an increased consumer market share measured by retail and consumer audits.

Several of our product innovation strategies and successful sales models implemented in East Africa were subsequently adapted and introduced into markets in West and Central Africa. We directly coached and trained over two thousand young people to be corporate salespersons, with many of them now employed in senior executive roles.

Our model was also good for the informal market retailers. They no longer needed to travel daily to wholesalers to source stock because, in most cases, it was delivered directly to their stores. Wholesalers began to lose their stranglehold on the markets, as suppliers were now demanding to know who their customers were and building tools to speak and sell directly to the clients.

The mobile apps we used produced incredible amounts of daily transaction data that allowed financial organisations to get a feel of the retailers' performance. That data allowed the institutions to offer daily credit to the informal markets based on the stores' historic trading performance instead of the need for capital-based collateral.

Our model was aimed at creating a "sales pull" environment, where the informal market dictated the consumer requirements and placed the order for the salesperson to fulfil. The focus then shifts from constantly looking for orders to managing the supply chain.

Predictability is the cornerstone of successful selling in informal markets. If you want success, longevity and sustainability in the industry, you need to master creating a "pull" environment for your product where the retailer knows you, knows your product, and wants to order your product. With that setup your duty as a salesperson is simply managing the relationship with the customer, keeping them informed and managing the supply chain.

I have read a lot of books on the art of selling and most are written from a Western market perspective. Although the content is helpful in some cases, it fell short when it came to addressing the opportunities inherent in African informal markets.

African informal markets are a misunderstood, dislocated, untaxed and an un-unified multi-billion-dollar industry. It is my hope that this book will give you greater insights into selling to Africa's informal retailers and help you identify and leverage the opportunities within the market.

1

UNDERSTANDING
INFORMAL MARKETS

THE GENESIS OF AFRICA'S RETAIL INDUSTRY

Rural-Urban Migration

Before colonisation, most Africans lived in rural village settings as family clusters under chieftaincy structures. In these settlements, they thrived on subsistence farming and exchanged goods and services using barter trade. The size of one's family and the quantity of livestock they owned in a kraal determined a family's importance.

As the family unit expanded, inter-community marriage continued the expansion of the families, with several children adding to the numbers and the consequential internal labour increasing the homestead's productivity and justifying the allocation of more land, while increasing influence within the community. No family or family member fell behind unless they were ostracised. Everyone had food, everyone had land and everyone had a chance.

As urban settlements developed during the periods of early African colonisation, family members (especially youth) left these rural communities to seek a new form of wealth creation: work-for-pay. The allure of capitalism and individual wealth, independent of the clan, drew thousands of African youths to urban centres. Rural-to-urban migration became commonplace, causing rural family structures to break down as family members left the homestead. This drastically reduced the labour force, which was previously the bedrock of the rural economy.

The emigration from rural areas left several homesteads with only the elderly parents tending to a few animals on a patch of land with little to no support. Because of age, they no longer had the energy to till the land or the stamina needed to utilise the draught power offered by the animals. The effects of the changes relegated the elderly to mere recipients of assistance from the children in urban centres.

Urban centres experienced significant population growth as people migrated to these areas, which were seen as opportunities for economic advancement. The availability of transport links, minerals, water sources, and trading centres played a key role in attracting populations and facilitating the development of towns and cities.

As these populations increased, centres of influence started to emerge within them.

While the old African drawcard for settlements was related to the availability of arable land, pastures, water and security, the primary pull for post-colonial settlements was capitalism. Yes, safety, arable land, pastures and the location of dams, rivers or lakes were still important, but now road or rail convergence points and proximity to other means of production like mines became strategically important. These centres of influence spawned support industries like restaurants, hotels and lodges, retail shops, salons, bars and many others. These industries only served to multiply the population numbers in the locations.

The old African traditional family structures required the youth to "wait" on their elders and to be under their patriarch and chieftaincy structures. In modern times, youth who were seeking opportunities would find little opportunity in those same rural models. They realised that money, which was now sadly the key measure of success, was not easily accessible in the rural areas and was always redirected to the patriarch. They became easily drawn to seeking employment in the urban areas with the promise of an easy quick buck and the trappings of wealth that they could see from colleagues who returned to the rural homestead every year during Christmas holidays. The symbols of success – cars, bicycles, portable FM radios, designer clothes and plenty of cash to splash at the village shops – lured more people to move to the cities.

With a dream of a better future in their sight, the rural youth arrived in the city with a goal to resolve the need for shelter, food, entertainment and companionship.

Once the issue of shelter was solved, they needed to look for employment to cover their expenses. To even have a fraction of those needs met, the young person was forced to integrate into the urban lifestyle consisting of shops, restaurants, cars, health centres, rental homes, salons, nightclubs, parks and other amenities.

The urban settlements became centres for the thriving exchange of monetary trade. Long gone is the old bartering and hierarchy of wealth that was common in rural areas. Reliance on family structures was no longer that relevant in the city. Success was measured by the favoured currency of the urban areas – money! The more money you had, the more assets you accumulated and the more friendships you were perceived to have.

Interestingly, the more successful you were in the city, the more influence you had back at your rural home, thereby disrupting the patriarchal structures. The one with more money now made decisions that in the past were made by the one with more years on earth.

This is a simplified overview of how informal markets developed and grew across the world. With this understanding, we shall therefore get into more detail on how to appreciate informal markets, their nuances and, more importantly, how to thrive and succeed in the markets.

> **Informal markets emerge where people and interests converge.**

HOW INFORMAL MARKETS DEVELOP

Having understood the African urbanisation genesis, it is easier to then appreciate how informal markets develop.

As young people and prospectors converge on an urban centre seeking opportunities, the first trigger for an urban settlement is a convergence of convenience.

Whether it is a network of roads converging, railway lines converging at a station, the confluence of a river or a river pouring into a lake, it is common to see increased populations centred around the area of convergence. In some cases, the convergence could be due to the existence of mining activity or security, like a hill. As the popularity of that centre of convergence increases, more people migrate to this new point and build houses and start businesses in and around those residences.

Across Africa, bus stations, water points and hills are the more popular convergence points for the beginning of an urban setting. Globally the same is true; train stations, bus stations, airports or water ports bristle with trade and influence urban developments. Small stalls selling foodstuff, groceries, fruits, vegetables and simple convenience products sprout in those convergence areas and serve those arriving or departing. Restaurants and lodges dot the area, as the new arrivals will always demand their services.

As the popularity of the centre grows, transport networks develop, connecting the communities huddling around the point of convergence. In no time, the demand for housing shall rise and the settlement shall grow. Some satellite settlements begin to sprout outside the main station. With a growing need for residential accommodation, it will not take long before municipalities are needed to control the progressive expansion of this urban community.

Because of demand, other industries open. For example, clinics and hospitals, vehicle repair shops, clothing shops, salons and beauty shops, and entertainment centres like bars and clubs start operating in the area.

As the industries grow, the demand for artisans rises, and they begin setting up their enterprises. Builders, painters, carpenters, electricians, plumbers and welders set up their businesses in the new urban centre to serve the needs of the communities and businesses in the area. Initially they would come from another town, do the work and return to base, but the growing demand for their services will force them to relocate to the centre or expand their business to the area.

Wherever humans are, there will always be a demand for products and services. Even pet breeders and pet food suppliers will have their space in the market. Everyone who is within and around the markets will find an opportunity to sell their product or service – all triggered by the original source of convergence and capitalism.

This book examines the retail industry with particular attention to the social, psychological, and environmental factors that contribute to the development of informal markets in Africa. We will take time to understand the distinct types of markets and how and when they morph into modern retail trade.

We have come to understand why, in some regions, the informal market may develop, grow, peak and then collapse; yet in other markets, they may expand, modernise and become structured, with malls, boutiques and supermarkets that integrate quality merchandising standards, point of sale technology and the use of modern selling technology.

What we need to understand is that settlement formations are organic, and their expansion requires a specific ecosystem to feed them. They develop their own culture and character, just like a person.

Being African, our informal markets share many similarities, with subtle differences distinguishing the settlements. As a salesperson, if your intention is to succeed in trading in these markets, you must appreciate each market's quirks, defects and beauties, and sometimes, it is important to understand "why" that urban sprawl exists in the first place to maximise your opportunity.

66

Today's admired modern retail in Western worlds started as small informal markets with the same store types and features.

99

THE STAGES OF RETAIL DEVELOPMENT AND THEIR TYPES

We have talked about how rural migration across Africa and the world was influenced by capitalism and how the convergence of conveniences caused the development of urban settlements and their supporting industries. Many people are born in cities or communities with already established retail facilities nearby, and it is hard for them to imagine a world without the current retail outlets, structured as they are.

It is hard for them to imagine a world without Mama Shaddai, who owns the kiosk around the corner. As kids, they would be sent to pick up a bottle of coke and mandazi to cater for visitors or the daily supplies of bread, eggs and milk.

It is difficult for them to picture a time when Shoprite or Chandarana supermarkets did not exist; shops where one would go and get groceries for the week – and not to forget every child's favourite moment of getting a sweet treat at the impulse shelves by the till point.

In conclusion, all retailing across the world starts off as basic informal trading but gradually becomes more structured, intentional and economically prosperous as the community becomes more economically empowered.

When we visit retail shops in Europe, we may be fooled into thinking they always looked like that, but they too had to develop from informal markets. I would summarise the progression of retail to start from a basic informal market structure, progressing to a developing structure and then to a mature structure.

Basic

All retail markets start at this point, whether in Africa or the Western world. Most of the African retail markets still have 90% or more of their market at this basic level of informal market trading, with tabletops, kiosks and small unstructured retailing. Consumers are exceptionally price sensitive, and their focus is on shopping for basics – the majority being foodstuffs. There is very limited focus on offering experiential shopping or value-adding, as it is assumed to only increase the cost of the product.

Consumers in those regions normally travel internationally to enjoy experiential shopping. Major retail chains and premium international brands struggle to gain a foothold in these markets and usually close after a few years of attempts because of the low footfall, low sales and constant cheap imitations that outsell them.

Developing

Several countries in Africa have or are expected to develop into middle-income economies. As the countries develop economically, their people have more disposable income, and their consumption patterns improve to demand more quality and improved retailing experiences.

Modern supermarkets, malls and internationally branded retail shops may grow to be about 30% to 50% of the overall retail experience, especially in the urban centres. Informal markets will remain about 50 to 70% of the retail economy centred around rural areas and high-density residential areas. Examples of countries across Africa that have achieved this status could be Kenya, Ghana, Zambia and Mozambique, just to name a few.

There will be an evident emerging shopping culture among the consumers that will see a rise in demand for experiential shopping. This will result in an increase in the number of speciality malls and retail chain shops that have kids' play centres, speciality restaurants, food courts, fast food chains, e-sport centres, movie houses, car washes and much more. As the number of consumers that want to experience international shopping in their own country increases, international brands and retail chains can be seen entering the market to test the demand.

Mature

A small number of countries in Sub-Saharan Africa have reached the mature stage of retail development. South Africa, Botswana and Namibia boast of a mature shopping culture.

In mature retail, the informal market will be less than 40% of the overall retail market, and different styles and sizes of modern retail malls and shops can be found across the entire country, including in the rural areas. The shopping culture is extremely formal, with strict guidelines on product quality and standards in force. If the bylaws do not control the quality look-and-feel, then the consumers and societies take matters into their own hands to demand structured order.

International brands become prevalent, with convenience and quality being the key purchase drivers for consumers. It is common to see retail promotions in newspapers, on television, on radio and in social media, boldly advertising crazy prices with stiff competition dominating the retail space.

The three stages of retail development do not indicate whether a country is socially successful or not. The dominant type of retail in a country is not a yardstick of the economy's performance, but it does indirectly give an indicator of the quality of the nation's infrastructure and the value of consumer living standard measures. As you will see later in this book, some African informal markets have resisted being overtaken by modern retail models.

Remember that every market has its own nuances, and the very thing that influences a market to emerge may be the one that determines whether it remains in its basic developing stage or grows to a mature state.

In conclusion, this retail evolution is synonymous with all retail markets worldwide and I am going to break down the market dynamics and clarify how retail informal markets can be better appreciated for selling.

A kiosk in the informal market

A shopping mall in Kenya

2

THE BUSINESS OF
INFORMAL MARKETS

THE INFORMAL RETAIL MARKET

At the start of an urban settlement, there will be limited to no formal municipal structures that direct the establishment of buildings, road networks, separation of residential from industrial areas, distribution of utilities like water and electricity or establishment of healthcare services. It is just an open piece of land that is ready for occupation, influenced by a convergence opportunity that will give rise to the establishment of communities.

The people in these new communities will initially live as they did in their rural homes – as families and relatives – and with time mix with other people from other areas. At this stage, everything will appear haphazard.

As in all societies, leaders will naturally emerge from the new settlers, and they will determine who gets land and in which area. Without a formal municipality mindset, that is where you may find industries within residential areas, disorganised road networks, or limited to no ablution facilities. The result is everyone will operate on a fight-or-flight basis within the community. It is rough, it is tough, and incomes will initially be low as the communities get to their feet.

As the number of residents in the area increases, they will need necessities closer to them, things like food, water, household goods, clothing and medicines, salons, transport, etc. Instinctively, industrious individuals will start to sell products and services from their homes and on street corners before doing so in more formal trading stores. This is not only a natural progression of retail in Africa but across the world.

I am going to build my talk on these enterprising entrepreneurial retailers. I will describe their different forms as they operate in the informal markets.

Hawkers

Hawkers are one of the first types of traders to operate in an informal market. Their business model is simple; they buy products in bulk from a wholesaler, break the packet, add a markup and sell their wares for profit as they walk around the community or a specific market area. On most occasions, they advertise their presence by shouting or making noise with megaphones or rattles.

Hawking is probably the largest employer in Africa and is a first option for male and female youth venturing into the informal market. You will find hawkers at traffic lights, at bus stops, at city squares, outside retail centres and at street corners. They are well known for employing distraction techniques to attract customers. They work hard, they work rough, and they make small but sustainable returns of about five to ten dollars per day.

Hawkers must be quick-witted and aggressive and have the resilience and fortitude to hold their place among their peers and competition. Most significantly, they are not taxed and not regulated across the continent, which is a huge loss of unmeasured and untracked GDP and a loss in taxation income.

Examples of hawkers that you will find in most African informal markets are:

- Those that carry a cardboard tray of individually stacked products like sweets, crisps, lollipops, cigarettes or drinks. What these traders do is buy full packets of their merchandise from wholesalers and sell them as individual pieces to commuters.

- Across Africa, it is common to see hawkers by traffic

lights and roadsides selling interesting impulse purchase products like ice cream, water, drinks and works of art for home decor. These hawkers or vendors are excellent in their target marketing and customer profiling, with direct engagement being their forte.

- In food markets and along high-traffic roadsides, it is common to see women sitting next to neatly stacked heaps of produce like tomatoes, onions and carrots and selling to passers-by and commuters. They normally target people returning home or going to work.

- In East Africa, it is not unusual to see beautician hawkers walking around with baskets of beauty grooming kits that include nail polishes and makeup accessories, ready to provide manicure, pedicure and haircare salon services to customers on the go.

- Then there are hawkers selling clothes, jewellery, shoes and accessories that they spread on the pavements or hang innovatively along roadsides for customers to try out and buy – especially in unregulated markets. In regulated markets, such hawkers, if they do not have permits, will always have their wares stacked in a way that makes them ready for a quick escape from the authorities. Interestingly, you will even see these hawkers on the streets of London and Paris! Informal markets exist everywhere in the world!

- In cities where food, health and safety regulations are more relaxed, fresh snacks like roasted maize, boiled eggs, roasted peanuts, fresh coconuts, roast meat, raw or cooked bananas and yams are sold by hawkers to commuters, targeting office workers, construction site workers, travellers using public transport and private cars.

Hawkers are very integrated into their communities,

giving them an innate way of identifying and serving the needs of their target clients.

The herd culture is extremely prevalent among the traders because the moment an idea is noticed to be working, several others will automatically adopt the same selling technique and sell in the same space, at the same price, using the same display standard. Intellectual rights and paper contracts do not have a place in this market. What counts most is hard work, grit, persistence and resilience.

In certain countries, manufacturers have taken advantage of the presence of hawkers to employ them as commissioned salespersons to sell ice creams, soft drinks, mobile phone airtime and more. These commissioned hawkers that sell on behalf of corporations would normally wear branded attire or use branded bags or trolleys that act as outdoor advertising while immediately dispensing the product at its immediate point of need – the final consumer. It is a very lucrative trade marketing opportunity for suppliers that I believe is still underexploited in most countries and can bring a lot of profit for businesses as well as generate profitable employment if implemented well.

Tabletops

Unlike hawkers, tabletop traders are more settled where they operate. They identify a location to sell from and display their wares on a small table from which they will sell throughout the day. They are typically positioned at street corners, particularly in residential neighbourhoods with significant pedestrian traffic and an increased demand for immediate home meal solutions.

Tabletops normally sell essential fresh produce like tomatoes, onions, fresh vegetables, sugar, salt, airtime, sweets and other condiments designed for a quick meal. It is quite common to see them sell commodities in small packs called penny packs or even break bulk and sell tablespoon quantities to families that are struggling – yes, they are an essential service at critical times. Tabletop traders are always in touch with the community and individual household needs.

As communities congregate at bus stations in the morning and evening rush hours, the success of hawkers, table-tops and open-air markets is dependent on how aggressive they are at their operational stations. While their market formations may appear random and haphazard, they are very structured to target the timely movement of commuters, and they have mastered the art of having the right product available at the right price when the opportunity arises.

Tabletops and Open-Air Markets

When tabletop vendors converge, they become an attraction, and we refer to them as open-air market traders. Open-air markets are a congregation of many tabletops and hawkers combined to trade, at times allocating themselves to sell in category-specific zones. For example, fresh produce, clothing, electrical and mechanical engineering traders are allocated separate category zones within the same market.

In places like Ikotun Market in Lagos, you will find all categories of foodstuff, including fresh meat, sold on the tabletops, which is quite common in West Africa. Open-air markets like that at Mbare Musika in Harare or Kawangware Market in Nairobi can be synonymous with produce sales as farmers bring their produce to the capital for wholesale redistribution across the city. These are markets that consumer and customer communities travel to, hoping to get the best possible bargain.

As open-air markets gain in popularity, more traders are attracted to the same informal market. The number and size of the tabletops increase as the volume of trade increases. As business grows, the tabletops begin to employ stall staff and commission-earning hawkers, whose purpose is to direct customers to the tabletop.

Regulation of the open-air markets is always a contested issue. Questions of who owns what position on the floor often result in disputes. If a vendor does not go to work on a particular day, their position may be taken, and fights or arguments may ensue as they seek to regain their spot.

While markets may start with community regulations, city councils and the local government will have to step in to set regulations, especially as the market grows. This inevitably leads to taxes being charged to vendors. Although the traders are not amused by the introduction of taxes and by-laws that come with councils, they tend to benefit from community amenities like toilets, sewage works and road networks.

Speaking of bylaws, if the council is not effective in enforcing the regulations, then gangs and nefarious groups will regulate the markets, leading to chaos and increased criminal activity in the marketplace and community.

Without laws, hawkers, tabletops and open-air market traders will sell their product using every trick in the book without paying attention to any harm they may cause. The selling of expired stocks and counterfeit products can also become rampant in such markets. Furthermore, the vendors may cause incredible noise pollution and block vehicular traffic as they sell or cook food along roadsides. In the name of selling and making a living, they will do it all.

Wholesalers

As hawkers and tabletops emerge in the informal market, wholesalers will normally be the first to notice the opportunity for replenishing the hawkers and tabletops with stock. They will establish themselves in a fixed structure, as close to the most active zone of trading as they can, offering bulk products at discounted prices. These wholesalers are usually individually owned and run by local business kingpins with significant financial and sometimes political influence in the community.

Traditionally, wholesales were the only way to get to the retail stores in informal markets with a ratio of about one wholesale to approximately forty informal customers. While this initially was convenient for manufacturers because they would only have to sell to a few wholesalers and meet their sales targets while having their product available across the informal market, this only benefitted the top-selling product manufacturers and was a critical disadvantage to smaller suppliers in their drive for national reach.

The product range carried by wholesalers was consistently limited, and wholesalers with greater influence exerted significant control over the manufacturers due to their bulk buying capacity. In time and intentionally, manufacturers have been focusing on directly accessing the informal market and circumventing wholesalers.

This was, however, with limited success, because wholesalers have made themselves an integral supply chain component of the informal market, and manufacturers remain very disjointed and unable to make enough impact to reduce the wholesalers' influence.

Today though, we have a greater presence of wholesale trading regions such as Kariakoo Market in Dar Es Salaam and Chikubo Market in Kampala, where you will find kilometres of road networks congested with trading businesses, carts and vans doing deliveries, and traders selling everything from hardware, farming products, foodstuff and more. The businesses are separated into specific category areas, so a buyer wanting construction materials, or mechanical equipment, or fabrics, or spices will know exactly where to go. Interestingly, most downtown shopping areas of major cities are becoming such wholesale centres, and their dominance is far from waning.

Kiosk Retail Outlets

Kiosks have different names across Africa, from 'spazas' in South Africa to 'window shops' in Southern Africa, 'tuck shops', or 'dukas' in East Africa. But we will call them kiosks in this book.

These are sometimes stand-alone metal or fixed building structures, booths or metal frame retail outlets that merchandise stock from inside and sell products from a little window with bars or fencing. The sales attendant stands behind the counter inside the shop and serves the customer from the small cutout window, and the customer is not allowed to handle the product before paying.

The retailers at this point do not trust the customer to handle their product for fear of damage or theft, so they prefer to use the little hole in the wall to conduct all trade, and they do not release stock until it has been paid for.

As tabletops generate more income, merchandising the product becomes a challenge. To avoid the daily arduous task of dismantling and replacing their displays on the table, they upgrade to a kiosk. In kiosks, the first traits of modern merchandising techniques begin to show, including an increased variety of products, a diversity of product categories to choose from, promotional displays and refrigerators for cold-chain products. Shelf-price advertising will not be available at this point, as the retailers will still not have enough competitive advantages to compete with the hawkers who may take advantage of and undercut the kiosk's displayed prices.

Most kiosk retail shops are within the compound of

the owner's house to avoid additional rental costs and are staffed by relatives or employees, while the owner of the shop will be at their formal workplace. Every end-of-day, some form of reconciliation of stock and cash management will be done. Rarely is digital selling technology employed in these retail stores, yet it would create immense opportunities for all stakeholders.

A few organisations have developed point-of-sale systems to track stock movement and merchandising for kiosks and small supermarkets in informal markets to track their performance and influence supply chain and logistics. I am personally optimistic that digitising small kiosks is the future for informal retail across Africa.

Their customers will always be from within the community (estate), and they will be visiting the same kiosk daily for their grocery needs. The customer and the retailer have a personalised relationship that may extend to the issuance of stock on credit for reliable customers, without the need for collateral.

Informal Supermarkets

As kiosks flourish, they will require additional merchandising space, additional personnel, additional stock, improved lighting and improved stock control, which brings in the introduction of till point devices and their operating stations.

At this stage, the retailer's trust concerns will need to be overcome, as the once reluctant kiosk owner is forced to allow consumers to walk into the premises and handle stock. The fear of theft, property damage and the potential loss of control within the shop is a major hurdle that the shop owner will need to deal with.

To avoid the incessant answering of the same questions now and again, the proprietor is forced to publish prices on the shelf, and inevitably, their competition starts to directly undercut them on their prices. The supermarket stage cannot be taken lightly because it brings with it a range of new challenges for the shop owner as well as for the customers.

In the early stages of supermarket development in informal markets, it is quite common to find overzealous security officers scrutinising every receipt at the store exit and wanting to match the product in the customer's shopping basket to the till receipt even if they had been watching the customer transacting by the tills. Security consequently creates bottlenecks at the exit, exacerbated by their total disregard for customer service, as all customers in the shop are treated as potential shoplifters. Yes, real losses happen from petty thefts and could lead to business closure, but normally, at this stage, the retailers' security fears tend to be exaggerated.

These supermarkets, as they get more successful, expand to have stock warehousing at the back of the building, quality gondola shelving for promotional product displays, a dedicated receiving bay and a dedicated till point zone with multiple point of sale machines. As time moves on, the supermarkets are staffed by buying teams, merchandising teams, additional till-point staff with the requisite till-point equipment and security staff.

Stock will be merchandised on gondola display units, and modern merchandising methods are employed to ensure that the product range in-house is displayed with a measure of calculated logic of category management and planogram management.

At this point, the logic of retailing is to buy stock at a lower price and sell it with a markup to make a profit. There will also be a focus on promotional activity to increase customer footfall. At this time, the retail space is not yet viewed as a profit centre.

With good vision and resources, some supermarkets will start to consider the aesthetics of the customers' shopping experience, like retail-tainment inside and outside the store, like in-store music, lighting management, painting and colour coding and fragrance management. The objective for supermarkets is simple: let the customer stay longer inside the store, let them walk through the entire store, and they will definitely purchase more products. This almost always works.

Today's supermarkets put a special focus on counting the traffic entering their stores as well as the flow (or movement) of customers inside the store. They encourage customers to walk throughout the store in pre-framed directions, creating the opportunity for impulsive buying by highlighting products at convenient sites across the store.

Most supermarkets add bakery and fresh delicatessen (deli) sections to the store to increase the appeal for more frequent daily store visits. The most sought-after basic products, like milk, sugar, eggs and bread, are placed deepest in the store to make sure that customers walk across the whole store, thus creating opportunities for impulse purchases of other products.

Modern supermarkets normally base their store layouts on the historical simulation of a mother's shopping habits. Research indicates that when mothers shop for groceries, they typically prioritise feeding their families first, followed by the household cleaning, before looking at other things like household upkeep. This behavioural pattern is mimicked in supermarket layouts, which often guide customers through fresh produce first, then fresh meat and bakery sections before leading to dry groceries, kitchenware, and finally laundry and cleaning supplies. In most cases, non-food categories such as pet products are placed at the back of the store.

While this is a simplified elementary overview of store layout structuring, today's contemporary store layouts have grown increasingly complex due to advancements in technology and understanding of category management strategies and objectives.

A mother, after selecting fresh produce, may move to cooking ingredients. Once the full meal preparation has been addressed, attention shifts to maintaining cleanliness, which makes it essential for customers to pass by detergents and hygiene products.

Finally, shoppers may browse areas featuring cookware and cleaning tools. Notably, detergents and soaps are intentionally positioned far from food items to prevent cross-contamination of odours. This arrangement is a fundamental aspect of retail planogram design, which is an entire book in its own right.

Leading retailers pay attention to the sensory environment, particularly focusing on scent and sound in order to enhance the shopping experience.

The aroma of freshly baked bread at the entrance, for instance, can stimulate impulse purchases among customers, especially those who are hungry. This explains why bakeries are often situated near store entrances.

Likewise, the fragrances found in the middle aisles, such as those from detergents and perfumes, encourage shoppers to linger and browse.

In previous supermarket refurbishments I facilitated in Kenya (for stores exceeding 1800 square metres), it was observed that unpleasant odours accelerated the pace of customer movement, thereby reducing both impulsive and planned purchases.

Therefore, maintaining rigorous cleanliness standards is critical. Spoilt meat and produce must be promptly removed from the store, and all cleaning equipment should be dried outside the store rather than under shelves. A continuous cleaning routine is required to ensure an optimal shopping environment for the consumers.

Where the kiosk's consumers are normally from the local community and buy for daily consumption, the average consumer in a supermarket tends to be from a longer distance, and their grocery basket is normally bigger, and their visit interval may be weekly. To deal with this mix of consumers, supermarkets have both shopping baskets and trolleys in their stores to allow consumers to load up in one shopping instance. Most successful modern supermarkets have vehicle parking facilities for shoppers and also provide security for vehicles. This gives their consumers peace of mind as they window shop and enjoy their retail-tainment.

The supermarket's ability to attract many consumers and boost grocery sales can invite the attention of manufacturers. Manufacturers will normally assign a dedicated key account salesperson to look after such supermarkets with specialised merchandising expertise and a focus on return on investment per square metre, which really is what profitable retailing is all about.

The success of some supermarkets may encourage the retail entrepreneur in the informal market to venture into opening more chain stores in other informal markets. Their success will depend on them having strong IT systems and controls within the business, a strong brand that attracts traffic into the stores and a special eye on managing their return on investment.

While informal markets may start with hawkers and tabletops, as they grow, they gradually improve their service and grow to be dominated by larger trading enterprises that include supermarket chains.

It is important to highlight that it is the consumer that ultimately benefits from the improved service and availability of quality products and a wide product range.

In the next section we will demonstrate how retailers

and suppliers can equally thrive from the unpredictable yet thriving informal market.

Modern Retail Chains and Hypermarkets.

In recent years, several major multinationals and publicly listed and venture-funded supermarket chains have emerged across Africa, including Shoprite Holdings Ltd, SPAR, Pick n Pay, Carrefour, Naivas, and Woolworths, to name but a few.

In the Southern Africa region, modern retail supermarket chains are more established with a strong heritage and contribute over 60% of the retail transactions nationally. In Kenya modern retail contributes around +/-40% of retail sales.

However, modern retail has failed to gain significant market share in most African countries, reaching only as much as 10% on average across all the retail trade. This means more than 90% of the retail market is informal.

Modern retail chains or hypermarkets are one-stop retail supermarket chains that tend to also be opened within well-defined destination locations, like a mall. These malls offer a number of shopping experiences, including groceries, clothing, electronics, household items, hardware, furnishings and many others.

Everything the consumer may need can be found under one roof in a single trip. The modern supermarket will normally be surrounded by supporting stores that offer alternative shopping experiences, like pharmacies, fuel stations, bookshops and restaurants. The supermarkets or shopping malls normally have ample parking spaces to cater for consumers coming from all areas of the city and other regions of the country.

Most shoppers at hypermarkets tend to buy enough groceries for an entire month at a time. Still, many also make weekly trips to pick up smaller items, often turning these quick visits into a fun family outing. Since visits are relatively infrequent, customers usually fill large shopping carts or trolleys with substantial orders. Hypermarkets regularly advertise competitive weekly promotions, featuring loss-leader pricing in newspapers and on television.

Loss-leader pricing is where retailers sell a specific range of products at cost price (or less) to attract customers to key products. The retailers are not fools; they recover the loss by charging considerably higher margins on non-promoted products, which happen to be the majority of the products in the store.

"

With a growing youth demographic, informal markets will continue to grow and thrive across Africa.

It is the quickest and simplest means of employment creation.

"

WHY DO INFORMAL MARKETS THRIVE ACROSS AFRICA?

Having explored how informal markets emerge and evolve in urban settings, it remains a striking paradox that they continue to dominate Africa's retail landscape. You would expect that as economies grow and quality of life improves, modern retail formats like malls, supermarket chains, and branded fashion outlets would naturally displace small supermarkets, kiosks, and table-top vendors. Yet, the opposite is often true.

Retail giants such as Shoprite, Pick n Pay, Metro, and Spar have made bold attempts to expand modern retailing across the continent, occupying space in big and small shopping malls. But many of these ventures have ended in retreat. For example, Shoprite was forced to exit several African markets, including Kenya, Tanzania, Uganda, and Madagascar, citing operational challenges and low returns. Retailers like Nakumatt, Uchumi and Tuskys, who dominated retailing in Kenya, closed entirely. Spar has scaled back its international footprint, choosing to refocus on its domestic market in South Africa.

So why do formal retail stores seem to be scaling back their roll-outs, while informal markets continue to thrive?

I have taken some time to understand why Africa's

informal markets continue to thrive even with the onslaught of modern retail roll-outs.

Convenience and Proximity

Informal markets are embedded in the daily rhythms of African life. They are located near homes, transport hubs, and workplaces. Consumers do not need to travel far, dress up, or navigate parking lots. The kiosk is just a few steps away. It opens early, closes late, and is always ready to serve the client.

Relationship and Trust

There is a personal connection between the buyer and the retailer. The kiosk owners know your name, your children, and your buying habits. You can negotiate prices, ask for credit, or request a smaller portion to suit your pocket without causing unnecessary drama. This relationship-based commerce is deeply cultural and resilient.

While modern supermarkets may remain dominant in some product categories and regions, informal outlets like kiosks and tabletops will continue to thrive. This is because consumers value the intimacy of contact with the trader and value the trust and convenience. They are not just buying products; they are buying relationships, reliability, and relevance.

Flexibility and Affordability

Informal traders offer products in quantities that match the consumer's budget. A spoonful of cooking oil, an onion and a tomato, or a single cigarette. These micro transactions are impossible in formal retail and extremely convenient for economies where unemployment is prevalent and the majority of jobs are informal.

Cultural Comfort

In a mall and in the formal market, some consumers feel judged. Right of admission rules apply, and consumers worry about how they look, what they wear, or whether they "belong". In a kiosk, there is no such pressure. You are among your people and face no judgement. You can buy a tablespoon of salt freely without attracting any shame!

Freshness and Transparency

Consumers believe that stock moves faster in informal markets. They can see the whole supply chain from the product being delivered, its freshness and the people handling it. There is a sense of immediacy and authenticity, unlike in big supermarkets where stock is taken from big doors written "staff only" and shrink-wrapped produce is stored in cold rooms where no one can see.

Informal Markets Are Lucrative

The adage "cash is king" rules in informal markets. Transactions are fast, frequent, and mostly outside formal banking structures. Traders prefer it that way. No taxes. No audits. Just trade. And manufacturers like informal traders, as they get their money instantly.

Mutual Reinforcement

About 85-90% of Africa's businesses are informal. Likewise, about 86% of all employment in Sub-Saharan Africa is informal due to the limited formal job opportunities (International Labour Organisation's 2025 Report). Most of Africa's working population earn their livelihood through informal channels, underscoring why informal markets remain central to both economic survival and consumer culture. Any player in the informal market naturally feels more inclined to support one of their own than give business to an unknown formal entity.

Political, NGO and Gang Influence

Unfortunately, informal markets are fertile ground for political influence and votes. By controlling access to basic services, politicians and gangs can sway votes and maintain power. We have seen examples of infrastructure built in informal markets like Kibera in Kenya, destroyed by goons for no apparent reason. NGOs, too, find endless causes to support in these markets, often recycling projects year after year without a specific end date or exit plan, all for their personal gains. Even foreign investors benefit from the chaos. In that disorder, they find profit, thereby encouraging informal markets to continue.

Modern Retailer Mistakes in Competing with Informal Markets

Interviews with executives from leading modern trade retailers across Africa reveal a common theme: misalignment with local consumer behaviour.

They admit that they underestimate how deeply rooted informal trade is. They built stores, but they do not build trust. "Their formats are too rigid. They could not compete with the agility of the spaza (kiosk or duka)."

Many people do not know that informal markets once existed in European countries, the Americas, Singapore and elsewhere. The fact is informal markets will remain dominant until governments develop formal structures that are profitably sustainable for all stakeholders.

When municipalities deliver services, enforce planning, and build accountable leadership, the informal markets will naturally decline, although they will never completely vanish. In Sub-Saharan Africa, countries like South Africa, Kenya, Botswana, and Namibia have made progress— but corruption and poor politics are sadly reversing the trend.

Roadside tabletops in Zimbabwe

Tabletop vendor in the informal market

> **66**
>
> Selling is the heartbeat of every business.
>
> **99**

THE IMPORTANCE OF SALES

No enterprise can exist without earning revenue or making sales. Whether it is for-profit or non-profit, every enterprise or business requires a source of income that funds its activities.

A non-governmental organisation needs donor or agency funding to pay for all its activities and staff and maintain its vehicles. The organisation must therefore sell its ideas to donors (send written proposals) in order to get funding.

On the commercial side of things, a retail store needs product sales to be able to pay for new stock, pay staff expenses and pay overheads incurred during its operation.

Therefore, the survival of any enterprise depends primarily on its source of income. That is why, by statutory law worldwide, the first line of all accounting is always donation, sales, income or revenue. Every line after that is an expense line that is consuming against that donation, borrowing, income, revenue or sale.

Sales figures are so important that they are monitored daily as a critical health check of any enterprise's sustainability. Investors, employees, stock exchanges, banks, news reporters, executive management, employees, and government organisations are interested in knowing the sales figures.

Mainstream business news focuses on corporate quarterly earnings. Business pitches often begin by outlining past sales performance, future trends, market sentiment, and expectations based on sales results.

When sales or revenues increase, both businesses and governments tend to increase investment and spending, respectively. Optimism rises, leading to bull markets in stock exchanges.

When sales decrease, organisations reduce staff and implement budget cuts. In response, the stock prices fall as investors offload shares of low-performing companies.

Low sales in private companies affect the amount of tax collected by governments. We have seen several African governments struggling to deal with social unrest primarily because they are failing to generate enough tax revenue, borrow or get donor income to meet their burgeoning expenses. So, focusing on growing the income, increasing revenue or funding is critical; otherwise, the resulting unrest will cause them to lose votes in the next round of elections.

Although sales, selling and revenue are that critical to any organisation, the sales departments and revenue agencies in Africa often receive little focus. Corporate sales should be recognised as a critical business function, deserving more training, time and resource allocation.

In the next sections of the book, we shall take time to appreciate the drivers that influence physical (not online) selling or income growth, and the steps executives must take to influence that growth through their staff.

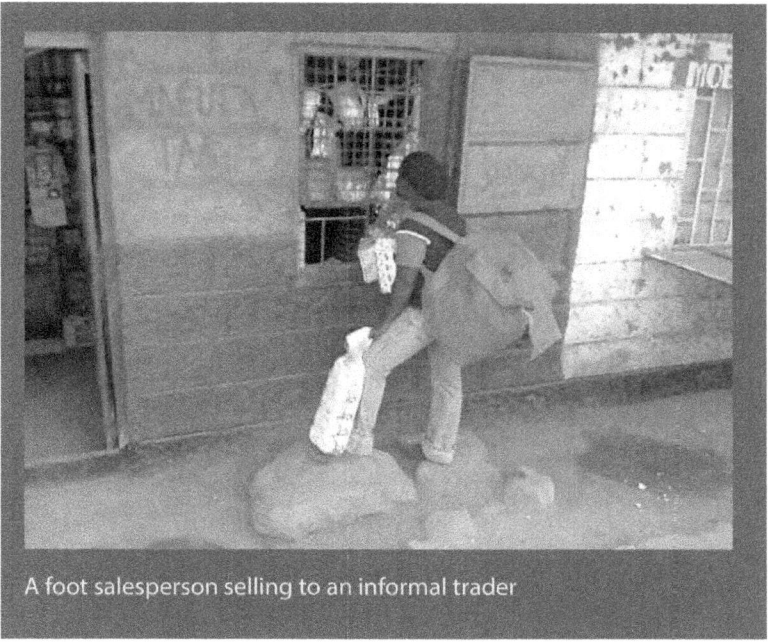

A foot salesperson selling to an informal trader

> **Profit is the primary motivator of the informal trade.**

THE CORE DRIVER OF CORPORATE SELLING

Selling in any informal market successfully and consistently across Africa is hard work. The competition is brutal and physical. You must be quick-witted, good with your words, cunning and always have another set of eyes at the back of your head. Sometimes, it feels as though, if you are not dirty and sweaty at the end of the day, you did not hustle enough. That is the impression the markets give you at first sight.

As you invest in the market, you will realise there are patterns in the way the informal markets work, and, just like a river, if you flow with the tide, you will be successful without experiencing hardship, strain and stress. If, however, you go against the patterns, the experience will not be pleasant.

There are so many variables that can influence one's success in selling in informal markets. The type of product or service sold, the timing or seasonality of the sale, the positioning and visibility of the product, the pricing of competition, the salespersons' selling ability, and the weather are all important variables that determine the number of sales one makes. However, there's a single primary factor that plays a pivotal role in determining the success of informal market trading; profit.

Profit

Individuals participating in the informal market engage in trading as a source of income, with profitable transactions being the main goal of their activities. Profit is the universal goal that drives the market. When making a sales offer, ensure it is profitable for both your company and the other party. This approach increases your chances of securing multiple deals.

If you focus on discussing issues about your company's values or the product instead of attending to the trader's need to maximise profitable earnings, you are wasting their time. Selling fails in informal markets when attention shifts away from the trader or when you become an added cost (wasting time) with no clear benefit. In such cases, traders will not engage, and your efforts will be unsuccessful.

As an aside, have you ever wondered why, when the city councils or government agencies build quality market centres for informal markets, the structures are quickly abandoned soon after opening?

The traders reject the stands en masse, preferring to sell outside the complex right in the mud and squalor. The reason for this is simple: traders are not interested in paying any additional fees for a service, even if the service is pertinent to the economy and the environment, as long as they cannot see a related upside increase in their profits. Whatever facility is built must tangibly attract new customers and increase the potential for profitable sales to see them scramble for trading space in the new venue.

In summary, quick and continuously profitable sales are what all traders in informal markets are looking for. That is the key driver for informal markets. The more profitable the sales are, the more informal market traders replenish their stocks and increase their investments in the enterprises. Their quality of life may also visibly improve as they upgrade their investments, which is important.

To achieve profitable selling, there are two important factors that every salesperson must know in order to guarantee that they are best equipped to succeed in their sales pitch. We shall delve into these in more detail.

Profitable Sales = Price x Volume

Where

Price = cost of the product + profit margin
Volume = quantity of sales

> **Small margins can sink a big dream.**

THE DRIVERS OF PROFITABLE SELLING – PRICE

Suppliers should recognise that, in addition to selling the features, advantages, and benefits of their product or service, the sales can be directly affected by the selling price and its relationship with the cost of the product. This, though, is not entirely in the control of the salesperson.

For example, charging too much of a profit margin for a product or service may make it uncompetitive versus the competition and result in loss for the trader or salesperson's sales. On the other extreme, charging too little margin on a product or service may make the product more desirable to consumers, but without making enough profit, the business is left vulnerable and may not cover its costs.

For suppliers and retailers, the selling price is typically determined by either the business owner or a dedicated finance or management accounting team, depending on the size of the business. The purpose of setting the appropriate selling price is to help maintain company profitability and fulfil requirements for corporate governance. In practice, the selling price of a product or service can be calculated using one of three methods:

Cost-plus pricing

This is the most usual form of pricing applied by most businesses, especially for pricing commodities or fast-moving groceries. It involves businesses adding the total cost of making the product or service to the minutest of detail, factoring in all aspects of direct costs. This means that they add all raw materials costs, shipping and supply chain costs, labour charges, any utilities like water and electricity, any licensing and taxes payable and any financing charges. Also added are some indirect costs like rent. Once the total cost has been accurately determined, a fair markup is added to the cost to determine the final selling price and discount, where relevant, of the product or service.

Most industries have predetermined fair margins that they adopt per product or service, and it is common in most FMCG (Fast Moving Consumer Goods) industries. It is always recommended that businesses be bullish in their setting of profit margins to ensure the recovery of indirect expenses like marketing, rental, financing costs, indirect staffing expenses and growing the cash balance.

Without looking at the volume consideration, businesses can succeed or fail on the profit margin set for their products or services. When profit margins are set too low, you will discover that within a few months, the business will already be swimming in cashflow challenges, and then the net losses creep in until the business no longer has any choice but to close. On the other extreme, if the profit margin is set too high, the product or service will be too expensive for the customer in comparison to the competition, and that may impact on the volume.

Opportunistic pricing

This approach considers production costs but sets the closing price higher to reflect anticipated market demand or the product's premium positioning.

For example, a premium coffee product may be introduced during a festive season. While the market may expect standard coffee to be priced at ten dollars, this special limited-edition package could be offered at twenty dollars for a limited period.

In informal markets, opportunistic pricing often occurs

during shortages, especially of essential commodities. For instance, if sugar becomes scarce and was previously sold at two dollars per packet, businesses may increase the price to four dollars solely due to the prevailing shortage without any changes in packaging or ingredients.

This practice allows businesses to mitigate the risk of depleting stock and addresses the higher costs required to replenish inventory, commonly referred to as 'replacement costing' in retail. By immediately adopting premium pricing, businesses engage in forward pricing to manage associated risks.

While such pricing strategies are widespread in informal markets, especially during periods of scarcity, they raise concerns about fairness, as they may appear exploitative against vulnerable consumers during times of need.

Penetration pricing

This pricing strategy is commonly used in service industries and can be seen in the FMCG sector. This approach involves significantly discounting a product or service, sometimes up to 100%, in order to reach as many customers as possible within a set timeframe. Penetration pricing is often used as a way of collecting customer information. Once the discount period ends or offer targets are met, prices return to standard levels.

For instance, a certain company recently introduced its e-commerce service to retailers in informal and rural markets. As part of registration, retail customers were asked to provide personal, business, and financial details through an app. In exchange, clients received free delivery for their first ten orders on top of promotional discounts on selected products.

This initiative attracted several retailers due to lower delivery prices than those available elsewhere in the market. The introductory offer was time-limited, and the company sold at a net loss during this period. However, the company obtained a database of customers for future engagement and gained insights into their requirements. While selling at a penetration price may cause short-term accounting losses, it can serve as a method for developing future business opportunities and gathering valuable data assets.

Who determines the selling price?

In a corporate environment, it is rarely an option for salespersons to influence or determine the selling price of a product or service. That is usually reserved for management accounting and finance personnel. These are people who understand the impact of price changes on the sustainability of the enterprise.

For small independent businesses, it is usually recommended that they invest in an external expert to assist in coming up with a sustainable selling price. Getting it right the first time is the first step to establishing a viable enterprise.

Although salespersons do not set the prices, it is important for them to have some level of flexibility on the selling price in the form of pre-set discounts. Sustainable enterprises must balance the need to set affordable and fair selling prices with sustainable profit margins on their products and services (which are not subject to change or manipulation once they are released onto the market).

A foot salesperson selling to an informal trader

A foot salesperson selling to an informal trader

" One sale is luck: Multiple Sales Are Strategy. **"**

THE DRIVERS OF PROFITABLE SELLING - VOLUME

The second driver of sales revenue, which is within the control of the salesperson when selling to informal markets, is sales volume. In informal markets, corporate salespeople are generally expected to sell as many units of products or services to as many trading customers as possible, on a recurring basis. The assumption here is they have access to retail trade customers, suitable products, appropriate selling knowledge, competitive pricing, and effective toolkits. While salespersons may not typically set the selling price, they do influence sales volume.

Growing Your Sales Volume Starts with Knowing Your Market

Just like building a house requires a strong foundation, growing a successful sales operation begins with solid groundwork. Long-term sales growth only happens when you clearly identify the markets where your product or service will be introduced.

In informal markets, this means understanding where your potential customers are located, estimating how many exist in each area, assessing market size and opportunity, identifying retail types, and collecting other useful data. This helps you make smart decisions, since you now know which areas are worth investing in and which ones may not be viable.

Finding the Sales Volume Rhythm – Mapping and Routing the Informal Market

When most people walk through a bustling informal market—think of Gikomba in Nairobi, Kariakoo in Dar es Salaam, or Mbare in Harare—all they see is chaos, stalls packed tightly like Tetris blocks, hawkers shouting prices, handcarts weaving through crowds, and dust rising with every step. It is loud. It is unpredictable. It is intense.

But if you pay closer attention, if you stay long enough, you'll notice the rhythm. The same vendors show up at the same spots. The movement of people follows invisible patterns. There are peak hours and quiet ones. Certain products cluster together—hardware on one end, tomatoes and onions in another. It is not chaos. It is just an unfamiliar order.

As sales professionals, our job is not to impose structure but to uncover the one that already exists. And that begins with mapping.

Lessons from the Field

In my early selling days, I was assigned a team of sales reps in a specific region. Back then, we did not have advanced mapping tools or employ tactical selling techniques. I made rookie decisions—dividing territories based on rough maps, hearsay, and gut feeling. Each day, we gave stock to the salespeople, who had to sell and reconcile it using handwritten invoices and leftover stock in their vans. An administrator would compile the results, and we would judge their performance from there. It was a hit-or-miss system, driven by massive Excel sheets and professional guessing.

Some reps hit their targets with ease. Others struggled and gave endless excuses. But one salesperson stood out—he always returned to base with an empty van, having sold everything. His numbers always balanced, and he became the star of the team and darling of the management. Then one day, he did not show up for duty, and upon investigating, we learnt he had been recruited by another company.

To fill the gap, we sent multiple salespeople to his route, but none of them came close to his performance. In fact, we could not even locate half the shops he used to serve. That was my first real lesson: if you do not map your retail outlets, record their contact details, and track their performance, you are flying blind.

Mapping is thus the foundation of volume selling, especially in informal markets. Know your opportunity, know your customer and build from there.

> **"** What looks like chaos is just an order you do not know yet. **"**

MAPPING INFORMAL MARKETS – WHY KNOWING THE TERRAIN MATTERS

The Hidden Order: Why Mapping Matters

Years ago, I worked with a juice brand that was trying to break into the informal markets of Nairobi. The company had a robust product, solid pricing, and aggressive targets. They deployed sales reps armed with smartphones and price sheets, but the results were disappointing.

The problem? No map, no real understanding of who the retailers were, what they needed, or even where they were located. As a result, sales reps wasted time walking in circles. Some outlets were visited five times in one week; others not at all.

We then realised we needed to take a step back and start from scratch—not by flooding the market with the product blitzes, but by just first understanding the dynamics of the market and listening and observing first.

A map was essential. Mapping, especially in informal markets, is not just about putting dots on a map. It is about building intelligence. It is understanding who sells what, when, and to whom. It is knowing which kiosks are run by the owner and which are rented to a cousin. It is spotting which parts of the slum are safe and which are crime hotspots after dark. You cannot Google that kind of information. You must be on the ground.

The Fieldwork Begins

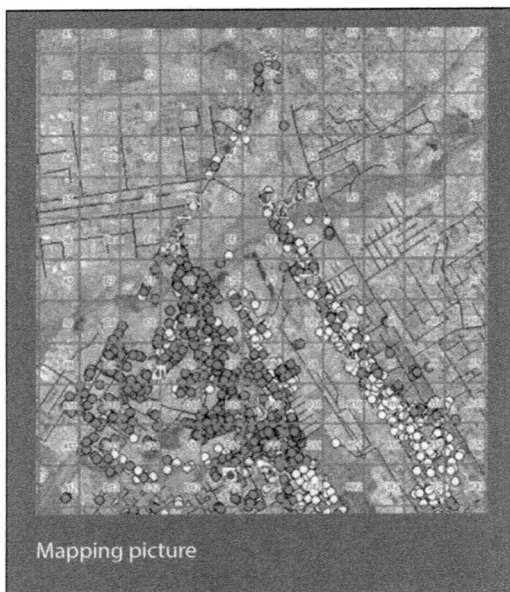

Mapping picture

We recruited a small team, all of them familiar with the area. Some were former delivery riders. Others had grown up in the very neighbourhoods we wanted to enter. Their job was to walk—kilometre after kilometre—identifying every retail outlet. From tabletop vendors selling sweets and chewing gum to small kiosks that stocked snacks, detergents, and soda. But it was not as easy as just walking in and asking questions.

Retailers in informal markets have grown cautious. Many had had their fingers burnt before, after being tricked into giving their phone numbers to organisations that later spammed them or, worse, sold their data. In Kenya, there had been multiple reports of small business owners receiving fake loan messages or falling victim to fraud after sharing their contact details. So, we had to earn their trust.

We approached the traders in a different way by telling

a compelling story—one that made sense for them. We explained that mapping would help us deliver faster, offer better promotions, and reduce the chances of them running out of stock. Our team dressed smart but simply, spoke the local slang, and often opened dialogue with some humour or small talk. Slowly, doors began to open.

Fieldwork in Reality: The Safety Lesson

There is another project that stays with me to this day— not because of how many outlets we registered, but because of how much it taught us about the importance of security in informal markets.

A client approached us with a bold request to help them launch their product in an informal settlement notorious for crime.

It was an area riddled with poverty, was congested, and was unpredictable in all aspects of life. Worse still, we learnt that about 10% of the slum was classified as a no-go zone; even local police avoided that area.

We took the assignment for two reasons. Firstly, the product itself was genuinely useful for the community and was needed. Secondly, we saw it as a chance to learn and serve an overlooked market.

So, the first step we took was to tap into local intelligence. One of our consultants who was born and raised in that very community proved to be important in our venture. We elevated him immediately, giving him new responsibilities to help with local introductions. He led us to community elders, influencers, and even the youth leaders—groups whose approval we needed before setting foot into the area. Only after being assured that we would be received in peace did we proceed.

Next, it was time to recruit staff. We deliberately hired sales reps from within the community. People who understood the dynamics of the area better than any outsider could. We trained them and gave them contracts while emphasising not just the technical selling skills but personal safety. We made sure everyone understood that safety always came first.

Then came the turn of the leadership to visit the area on a familiarisation tour. During my visit, which was done on foot, I remember walking past a coloured pole lying on the ground. There was nothing odd about the pole until I heard a voice behind me—a young man chatting on his phone.

"How much will you pay for a Samsung that is in perfect condition?"

He was asking someone how much they would pay for my phone. I then recalled pulling out my device a few minutes earlier to check something.

He was looking at me now, not menacingly, but with a faint smile – probably checking if I got the hint. I smiled back, made a light-hearted joke, and discreetly signalled to my team to turn around and retreat. Only after passing the coloured pole did one of my teammates inform me that we had unknowingly crossed into the red zone—one of the areas we had been warned not to enter because of safety issues. As I sat in the car after getting home, I reflected on the incident and realised it was indeed a close call.

That project, despite the initial scare and security concerns, ended up being one of the most successful initiatives we ever ran. In six months, we registered and activated over three hundred new outlets. But the lesson stuck. From then on, we embedded personnel safety into every single market mapping and sales policy we designed.

Whether it was a slum, a village, or a peri-urban zone, we now made it a priority to study the red zones—places made dangerous by gang activity, drugs, flooding, or complete inaccessibility. Sometimes it is the riverbanks that flood or rail tracks that divide safe zones from risky ones. Whatever the case, we learnt to map risk the same way we mapped opportunity.

Crafting the Conversation

Every survey we conducted was designed like a conversation, not a stiff interview. We asked the retailer to tell us the products they sold, how often they restocked, which suppliers they liked, and what challenges they faced. We kept it short—no more than eight minutes per store. Time is money in the informal market, and a customer might walk up mid-conversation and change everything.

The mapping tools we used were mobile apps with GPS tracking. Each store's location, photo, and basic details were recorded. Even the ones who declined to participate were noted—with just a name, location, and store type.

You never know who might change their mind next month.

Before we finalised the mapping tool, we had to test it out ourselves. We walked with the team, timing each visit, correcting awkward survey questions, and making sure the process flowed like a natural conversation.

The goal was always efficiency—get in, get the story, build a relationship and move on.

The Power of the Map

Once we completed the mapping, we had something no competitor had: visibility of the market. We knew every corner shop, every roadside table, every dusty shack that had the potential to carry our product. And from that information, we could finally build a selling machine.

That is where routing came in.

Routing is where planning meets practicality. If mapping tells you where the customers are, routing tells you how to reach them efficiently.

Building the Sales Engine

With two thousand mapped outlets in one suburb, we now had to figure out how many salespeople we needed and how they would move. We calculated how long it took to visit a shop—on foot, with a bike, or using a motorbike. We factored in breaks, traffic, and even market days. We discovered that, on average, a single rep on foot could comfortably visit 28 outlets in a day. That is one hundred and fifty-four outlets a week if they worked six days in a week.

But not all outlets were equal. Some barely moved product; others placed weekly orders. So, we split the list: high-potential outlets were visited every week, mid-tier outlets biweekly, and low-potential ones at least once every quarter.

We made deliberate decisions to avoid wasting time in places that did not fit our product. For example, if a hardware store did not want to stock juice after five attempts, we moved on. Although the outlet remained on our radar, it no longer ate up valuable time. Our resources had to match the return.

Adapting Delivery to Terrain

In dense settlements, reps worked on foot or with bicycles or used small motorbikes for delivery. Their drop sizes were small—between ten and fifty dollars per stop—but the volume added up quickly as they moved. We then created mini distribution hubs where the sales reps could collect fresh stock mid-route.

In more spread-out regions, motorbikes and tuk-tuks made more sense. Although the cost of operating was higher, yes, but it paid off in speed and coverage.

Larger outlets like wholesalers or supermarkets were serviced by trucks. But often, those big deliveries were triggered by the small sellers—our feet-on-the-ground sales reps—who would collect orders during their rounds.

The Invisible Foundation

From the outside, all these efforts looked like slow progress, given there were no sales yet. Just walking, talking, planning. But under the surface we were making tremendous progress, and the invisible groundwork would one day make all the difference.

Mapping gave us knowledge. Routing gave us direction. Filtering gave us focus. Altogether, they gave us the ability to build volume sustainably and predictably.

When we finally launched full-scale sales into the mapped territory, our hit rate was incredible. Reps were not walking in blind anymore. They knew the outlet, the owner, and the previous response. They were armed with information, with strategy, and most importantly, with confidence.

Reflections from the Field

I have seen too many companies fail because they jumped into informal markets with no map, no training, and no plan. Then when things collapsed, they blamed the salespeople, or the market, or the economy.

But the truth is, informal markets are like rivers. They flow with or without you. If you do not understand the course, you'll drown. If you do and respect it, you will ride the current to success.

We did not conquer chaos. We partnered with it. That is the secret to growing volumes in the informal market.

"

Cash is the king in informal markets.

Credit is the hidden goldmine of opportunity.

"

BENEFITS OF SELLING TO INFORMAL MARKETS

Across Sub-Saharan Africa, today's boardroom leaders continue to under-invest in their biggest selling opportunity, which they ironically see daily as they drive to their offices. There are several benefits to selling to the informal market segment.

Cash Business

While today's modern supermarkets and wholesale traders will order in bulk for all their chains, this usually comes at a price of heavy discounting, extended credit of up to ninety days and power jostling negotiations. In contrast, the orders informal markets take are in cash, with no discounts and limited negotiations.

Consumer Habits

Informal markets offer their local consumers personalised service, credit in tough times, free delivery, perceived quality, perceived pricing advantage and neighbourhood facilities that supermarket chains cannot.

While consumers may visit the supermarket chains for their weekly or monthly bulk needs, they often turn to kiosks for their daily perishable needs of fresh fruit, vegetables, perishable dairy and light top-up grocery. Those on limited budgets can commonly buy single use sachets and servings of grocery items with ease.

Suppliers who understand this trend will gain sales and market share from ensuring they have the right pack-sized products and product range for the retail outlets.

Direct Marketing

The local informal trader is usually a trusted local resident of an area. On some occasions, they hold positions of influence of some kind. As a supplier, they are an effective ambassador of your product. Sitting directly at the point of purchase, they elicit qualitative and quantitative responses on consumer opinion to your product and its competition. If you train the informal trader on your product, they become your best "free" ambassador.

Number of selling opportunities (translatable volume)

The number of modern trade stores in most sub-Saharan countries does not exceed a few hundred. Even though they order impressive volumes per store, there are only a few of them to deal with. On the other hand, informal market outlets number in the thousands, and their quantity translates to direct volume of sales. This metric reflects the level of opportunity inherent in all informal markets.

Affordability

There has been a lot of analysis on the disproportionately high cost of delivery in the last mile in Africa, but almost all that analysis tends to focus on delivering to the rural areas where the terrain is vast and the on-the-ground spread of the retail points and the value of drop sizes do not offer a financially viable supply chain return.

A few companies, notably Copia Global, tried and succeeded in reducing the cost of the last mile of delivery to rural areas, although they later shut down due to other venture capital-based issues. With delivery to informal markets in urban centres, the opposite happens. Retail points are concentrated; you have road networks and suitable infrastructure, and the drop sizes per store are encouraging, thereby reducing the delivery costs per drop. The main challenge in Africa, though, is the limited availability of delivery addresses. Several companies, and especially e-commerce companies like Jumia and Wasoko, have, however, had incredible success in urban delivery, and this was after solving the supply chain last-mile cost of delivery.

Automation

The advent of real-time mobile reporting in the informal market has allowed all the listed stores to be like one giant supermarket on the dashboard of a single supplier.

You can analyse all types of reports from personnel management, retail sales, regional performance and product selling reporting, just as you do in modern trade. It can become a unified marketplace.

Without diminishing the growing modern trade influence across sub-Saharan Africa, the informal market must be a more positive addition to the bottom line of any organisation's revenues. The opportunity is real.

66

Innovative mapping and software can unify informal retailers into a single, data-driven marketplace; unlocking exponential growth and investment potential.

99

THE MULTIPLICITY OF VOLUME SELLING IN INFORMAL MARKETS

As we have already highlighted, the informal market is often dismissed as chaotic and unpredictable, but it is a powerhouse of consistent cash-based transactions. When approached with structure, scale, and digital oversight, its potential eclipses many modern trade strategies. A practical case from Nairobi illustrates this remarkably well.

Justification for Mapping and Structured Selling

Some time ago we conducted a mapping and route planning exercise across Nairobi's informal markets for a client that wanted to increase their brand visibility. Modern trade was locked out for them because of the focus on category leaders and historic performance. The potential to get fair shelf space was limited, so their next best opportunity was growing in the informal markets.

From our mapping results, we identified twenty-six thousand relevant outlets that we could target for their diaper brand. From that list of retail outlets, we removed outlets with limited trading potential or capacity. This was either because they did not stock or trade the category or because they did not have the financial capacity to trade. This left us with a target of sixteen thousand informal retail outlets to visit, ranging from kiosks to tabletop and small supermarkets. We then assigned a team of fifty-two salespeople and designed route plans for each of them to ensure that all the outlets received at least one single visit per month.

The Maths Spoke Volumes:

- There were 26,000 outlets in the designated regions, and 16,000 of them were relevant for the products we intended to sell. We decided to focus on selling to those relevant outlets only.

- We timed how long it took for a salesperson to sell to an outlet and added the time for rest, travel and breaks. From that result, each salesperson was responsible for visiting 20 different outlets daily, working according to a set route plan for 6 days per week.

- Each store in our database of 16,000 was meant to be visited a minimum of twice monthly. The most active stores received visits twice weekly; less active stores were visited weekly, and others fortnightly, depending on the frequency of orders and potential of the retailer. Not every visit produced an order (we called that effectiveness), so we set a target for the salespersons to improve from a low of 20% effectiveness at the start to a peak of about 60 - 80% effectiveness within a period of three months.

- Orders from the shops ranged from $10 per visit with tabletops and small kiosks to $100 with small supermarkets and wholesalers. While there are many delivery models possible in the informal market, this client's model required the salespersons to pick up stock from a designated stock point and walk with it through their visits, immediately fulfilling the order. For bigger orders, they would have assistance from vans in the area.

- All the salespersons had to input(immediately upon completion) their transactions into our mobile app, and that meant we had an average of 36,000 transactions recorded every month. That translated to more than $360,000 of cash transactions against their stock deliveries being generated for our client monthly.

- From that information we could see orders by product, quantity and value per store, pipeline visits scheduled, missed or lost opportunities and immediate results versus the target in real time. We had the capability of putting up a screen with real-time results that we could follow up with the salesperson as they transacted in the field from the luxury of our office and simulate a control-tower coordination of our teams.

Within three months, the revenue we were generating was almost equal to what the client was selling through three modern trade retail chains on 90-day payment terms. And it did not come with the exorbitant cost of merchandising that modern retailers charge these days for just having a presence in their outlets. This project had a profound effect on our clients' liquidity and their visibility in the retail market. Of course, the consumer benefited from variety.

We continued to work with them for four years, growing their market until they were controlling the market share.

The best part of the informal selling model was that the selling cost that included sales representatives and supervision costs was under 15% of the income, and the total cost of selling was affordable in comparison with selling to modern retail chains.

This selling model is fully scalable. The multiplicity of growth is not speculative—it is visibly exponential.

In our example, if our salespeople generated $360,000 monthly for the client, then double that team, and you would generate $720,000, and likewise, a deployment of just ten salespeople would generate about $37,000 monthly.

Having statistics is important, as that helps you make informed decisions which make selling in informal markets viable and not haphazard.

Armed with the right numbers, you need to have the following things clear before you embark on selling to the market:

- You must designate areas with a suitable number of outlets that are concentrated enough for viability.

- You must assign salespersons to areas where shops are busy (money is changing hands). This is where there is a fair expectation of conversion of the sales into value (effectiveness).

- You need to have a good range of quality products and varying pack sizes ranging from small, medium and large packs.

- Your prices must offer fair profitability to the trader, and the product must have the potential of being sold out within a couple of days or weeks for maximised sales rotation.

When you have that dynamic firmly taken care of, you then calculate the cost of the salespersons and their commissions – which, to be fair, are not so dramatically high across Africa. The cost of the salespersons and the total project cost should ideally not exceed 15% of the total cost of selling in order to ensure that the project remains viable for all stakeholders. The manufacturer should get a profitable return, the salespersons should be paid on time and in full, and the retailer's trading should be profitable.

At these levels of multiplicity, informal markets are not "alternatives" for selling volume—they are economic engines.

The Management Myth: Risk and Resolution

Yes. There is an elephant in the room. As sceptics will often highlight, "Mass recruitment is risky." I absolutely agree with that fear, and I have the grey hair to prove it, but they are not entirely accurate in their assessment. Mass recruiting is not insurmountable if the right due diligence is taken:

Return on Investment

It goes without saying that with higher risk must come higher returns. So, you need to make sure that you recover enough profit in these operations to remain viable and to remain cash positive. The greatest risk is running out of cash in such operations because you are losing money to expenses.

Insurance Coverage

Ensure that you have a solid insurance package to cover theft, mass absenteeism, and gross mismanagement situations. There are several insurance policies that have been developed and can be adopted. You must ensure that the right checks and balances are in place to ensure that you follow their minimum requirements in the event of a claim.

Digitised Oversight

The use of mobile apps by the salespersons for all their transactions is an absolute necessity. We used to say, "No report, no pay." We only paid for sales that were from the app, and the only way to input into the app was when you were at the shop. Every transaction input was verifiable with actual delivery notes. Every sales rep's movement, outlet visits, and sales returns can be monitored in real time using mobile apps.

Predictive Sales Tools

With the data derived from the sales team inputs, you need to invest in analytics to remain on top of the game. Set up automated flags that go to the relevant managers and ensure that supervisors are always up to date with their teams' activities.

Simply put, the informal market needs better risk management and governance tools to be equitably viable for all parties.

Rollout & Market Mapping: Building the Sales Ecosystem

The informal market is not just a place to sell; it is a living, breathing system. Every kiosk, tabletop, and small shop is part of a bigger story. When we map these outlets with care, we do more than collect data. We build a network of trust, movement, and growth. Each visit adds value. Each transaction builds a relationship. Each sale brings us closer to something powerful.

This is not theory. It is real. We have seen it in action. With the right tools, the right people, and the right plan, informal markets can deliver strong cash returns, fast growth, and lasting impact. The numbers prove it. The stories confirm it. The results speak for themselves.

What starts as a route plan becomes a rhythm. What begins as a sale becomes a system. And what looks like a small shop becomes a key part of a national engine. This is the beauty of informal markets. They are not broken. They are waiting. Waiting for structure. Waiting for respect.

Waiting for someone to see their true value.

When we roll out with purpose and map with care, we do more than sell. We unlock a future. A future where African businesses grow from the ground up. A future where cash flows, jobs grow, and communities thrive. A future where informal is not second-best—it is the best place to begin.

Let us build that future. One outlet at a time. One visit at a time. One sale at a time. The opportunity is here. The time is now. Let us walk into it—with courage, clarity, and commitment.

3

THE SKILL OF SELLING TO INFORMAL MARKETS

DEFINING CORPORATE SALESPERSONS

Natural Selling

From the moment we are born, we learn how to ask for what we need. When a baby cries, they are asking for help; maybe they are hungry, wet, or feeling uncomfortable. The parent listens and responds, either with care or correction.

As the child grows older, they learn how to use words. They figure out how to ask in ways that get them what they want. But not all asking or crying gets the child what they want. For example, if a child throws tantrums in a shop to get sweets, later they may discover that this form of asking leads to trouble at home.

So, through experience, the child begins to choose the right time to ask and learns how to use their voice, their face, and their body to help them get a "yes".

As we grow, we also learn about trust. We learn that if we break trust, people may not listen to us next time. By the time we become adults, we will have already learnt how to sell our ideas and needs without ever going to a sales class.

Now let us look at examples of how different age groups sell their ideas.

A child might come home from a friend's house and say, "Mum, can we get that cereal with the lion on the box? It is so yummy! Amani eats it every morning, and he says it makes him run faster at football."

That is an example of a sales pitch and negotiation in one. That simple request shows excitement, proof from a friend, and a reason to buy, all in one sentence.

A teenager might say, "Baba, if I help clean the car today, can you take me to basketball practice later?" This is a deal. The teenager has offered something useful and asked for something they want in return. It is a clear example of a give-and-take exchange.

In adulthood, my friend Noel, who is just getting back from a weekend getaway, might say, "You must try this little lodge in Bagamoyo we stayed at. It is quiet, right by the beach, and the staff treated us like family. I did not expect much, but it was honestly the most relaxing weekend I have had in ages."

This is natural selling because he is sharing a personal and authentic experience. It is now for me to associate the lodge with my desires, leaving me with a curiosity to ask for more details.

Natural selling is less about persuasion and more about enthusiastic storytelling. It happens when people talk about a great book, a reliable mechanic, or even a parenting tip that worked wonders. The key is in expressing genuine belief in the value enjoyed.

No matter who we are, whether we are shy or outgoing, our success in life depends on how well we share our story. The more confident we are at storytelling, the more successful we are at attaining our needs.

People may say "no" to our requests. That is part of life. We must learn to keep trying, and we must get better at choosing the right time and the right way to ask, so we have a better chance of hearing "yes".

It is because of natural selling that many executives think anyone can sell anything. They believe that if someone is a good storyteller, they can also sell products for a company.

To an extent, yes, and most salespeople start that way. However, it is an error to assume that selling is straightforward.

Then there are some who believe that a product's quality alone guarantees sales. Then they hire sales personnel who are natural storytellers and focus resources on branding, advertising, and transportation, while overlooking the training of the sales team in the formal aspects of sales processes. This approach assumes inherent product appeal will ensure success. However, selling in informal markets involves more than just enthusiastic presentations.

Commercialising the transaction requires skills that must be developed. Decisions regarding your salesperson can determine whether your product thrives or fails in the market.

Individual Selling

It is one thing to be able to sell your personal car or house and another to sell the same things as your daily 8-5 job and earn a living from it. You may have a whopping success in selling a single item in a day, but will you manage to sell the same product or real estate property repeatedly to the same community of customers for a week, a month, or a year? Will you be able to successfully sell to the same audience day after day? The reality is that even your own family will turn you down on your second or third attempt to sell to them.

Individual selling is usually driven by an emotive rationale that influences the person selling to be more determined, committed and emphatic in their selling. As an example, if you need to clear a personal debt, you may decide to sell an asset. In the act of selling, you are motivated by the expected freedom from debt and will scarcely care about the potential for a future resale. You can afford to be as crass, nonchalant or rude as the situation demands. You can also make non-committal promises. You can dispose of the asset at a loss. Individual sales require only limited accountability, as the specific terms of each sale may vary according to subjective reasoning and emotional factors.

Corporate Selling

A corporate salesperson is responsible for promoting and selling an organisation's products or services to the retail market. What distinguishes corporate salespeople from individual salespersons is that the former are required to develop a database of relevant sales leads; they are to pitch their product or service and close sales transactions in the marketplace on a daily or weekly basis, with specific sales targets to achieve.

As an example, a ballpoint pen salesperson may have ten different batches of stationery pens to sell off monthly; that is, one hundred pieces per batch or 1,000 pieces to be sold every month. The pens are obviously more than the salesperson can consume personally and more than they can sell to their family and friends. The salesperson may initially try to sell the pens to people they know, but that may not be sustainable if they want to sell weekly or monthly.

To sell the pens, the salesperson could choose to sit by the street corner and call out to passersby like a hawker. But how many people will walk past that corner every day and will happen to have a need for those pens? Is the salesperson speaking to the right target audience?

A corporate salesperson must strategically visit enough traders routinely to sell their target quantity of pens, handling objections, restocking and ensuring they keep the trader profitable. They must reassure the traders of the promised objectives of margin and volume and ensure they give their support for continuous future sales transactions.

A corporate salesperson must strategically visit enough customers to sell their target quantity of pens to all the traders, handling objections and ensuring they close the deal. They must reassure the trader of the promised objectives (primarily profitability) to ensure they have their support for future sales transactions.

Corporate selling involves several disciplines aside from relationship management and selling. These include planning ahead or demand forecasting, managing or coordinating delivery logistics, negotiating, marketing and advertising, product and quality control management, managing debtors' collections and reporting. A corporate salesperson should coordinate these activities seamlessly. This book's focus is to share the corporate selling skills and tactics needed to succeed when selling to Africa's informal markets.

The Distinction Between Marketing, Selling, and Trade Marketing

So often I am asked what I do for a living. When I explain that I am into sales, I am met with a confident reply:

"Ah, so you are in marketing?"

It is a well-meaning assumption—but also a common misconception. While marketing and selling are intrinsically linked, they serve distinct but complementary purposes that shape how products move through markets, especially informal ones.

Marketing is about crafting perception. It shapes how a product is seen and felt by the end consumer, building emotional appeal and long-term brand value. Through branding, storytelling, and visual identity, marketing aims to cultivate desire, familiarity, and loyalty. Its focus is upstream—creating demand and forging a connection between the product and the person who will ultimately use it.

Selling (sales), by contrast, is the engine of movement. It is action-orientated, grounded in the immediate and transactional. Selling is about getting products into the hands of traders, retailers, and resellers. It transforms interest into revenue. In informal markets, it means navigating relationships, negotiating prices, and ensuring products are physically accessible at the right time, in the right quantities.

These two disciplines may speak to different audiences:

- consumers (the buyer to consume or use the product or service)
- customers (the buyer who shall resell the product for profit)

The Bridge

Sitting at the intersection of marketing and selling is trade marketing—an often-underappreciated powerhouse in the African informal markets, especially for the art of selling. Trade marketing is not about mass exposure or brand storytelling; it is below-the-line, tactical, and directly engages the channels that move product.

Rather than targeting the end-consumer, trade marketing targets resellers, distributors, and informal traders, the frontline agents of market access. It includes in-store promotions, point-of-sale displays, merchandising strategies, product training, and incentives that drive behaviour among these intermediaries.

When a salesman sells a product into the hands of a trader, it is important for that product to be sold out so that space to sell-in fresh stock may be created. That is the primary purpose of trade marketing, that is, to create the right environment for goods and services to be noticed by consumers and exchanged for value, at a profit.

Why Trade Marketing Matters

Trade marketing is how we help products move from the warehouse to the shop shelf—and then into the hands of real customers. It is not just about selling. It is about making sure that traders, retailers, and shopkeepers know the product, trust the product, and want to sell the product.

When trade marketing is done well, everyone wins. The manufacturer gets more sales. The retailer earns more profit. And the customer finds what they need when they need it.

Trade marketing focuses on the people who sell the product every day. These are the shop owners, kiosk operators, tabletop sellers, and small supermarkets. They are the ones who talk to customers, answer questions, and decide what to stock. If they believe in your product, they will push it. If they do not, it will sit on the shelf.

Trade marketing matters because it builds trust. When you visit a shop and explain the product, show how it works, and offer fair prices, the trader feels respected. They are more likely to give your product space on their shelf. They are more likely to recommend it to their customers. And they are more likely to reorder it when it sells out.

It also helps with visibility. In informal markets, there are many products fighting for attention. Trade marketing helps your product stand out. You can use posters, shelf talkers, branded shirts, or even small giveaways. These tools help the customer notice your product and remember it. When they come back, they ask for it by name.

Trade marketing also helps with education. Many traders do not have formal training. They learn by doing. So when you teach them about your product—how to store it, how to explain it, how to sell it—you are giving them skills.

These skills help them grow their business. And when they grow, your product grows with them. Another reason trade marketing matters is because it helps you understand the market. When your team visits shops, they see what is selling, what is not, and what customers are asking for. This feedback helps you improve your product, adjust your pricing, and plan your next move. It is like having eyes and ears on the ground.

Trade marketing also supports loyalty. When traders feel supported, they stick with your brand. They defend it when competitors come knocking. They become your ambassadors. And in informal markets, loyalty is gold. It is what keeps your product moving, even when times are tough.

Finally, trade marketing helps with planning. You can track which shops are selling well, which areas need more support, and which products are moving fastest. This helps you decide where to invest, where to expand, and where to improve. It turns guesswork into strategy.

In short, trade marketing is the heartbeat of retailing in informal markets. It connects the product to the people. It builds trust, drives sales, and creates lasting relationships. Without it, even the best product can fail. With it, even a small brand can grow into a household name.

A bicycle salesperson in Nairobi

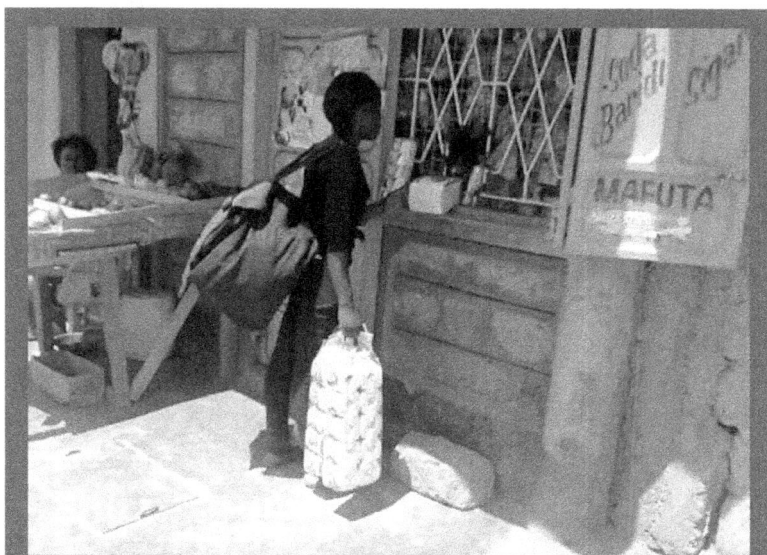

A foot salesperson selling to an informal trader

"The best salesperson is the one who will face rejection ten times and still pick themselves up for another shot at success."

THE SKILL OF CORPORATE SELLING

To succeed as a salesperson in informal markets, it is essential to understand local community dynamics and ensure your products are available, visible and accessible when demand arises. This involves strategic positioning and effective communication so that the customers know what you offer and the price.

In large cities like Nairobi and Dar es Salaam, the CBD population fluctuates between day and night because of commercial inflows and outflows of traffic. This creates a need for more than one hundred and fifty thousand retail shops and countless street vendors to serve the millions of consumers. Ensuring your product reaches every outlet and stays top-of-mind for consumers remains a significant challenge.

Traditionally, shop owners determine their inventory, with choices shaped by wholesalers who distribute products according to their own priorities. Manufacturing sales staff typically direct their efforts towards wholesalers, with limited influence over how products are ultimately delivered to consumers.

Technology is shifting this power dynamic. With tools like mobile tracking apps, manufacturers and their sales teams can now engage directly with informal market retailers and circumvent the wholesalers. This allows manufacturers to manage their products' availability and visibility in the informal retail and offer greater variety to consumers. Retailers benefit from this model because they do not have to leave their shops in order to restock. In tandem, the consumers gain by having access to more choices at better prices.

Selling core driver

These core driver's tend to change when a salesperson visits a modern retail chain. Modern retail's focus is not only on the product's profitability but more on the return-on-investment of the shop's floor space.

In modern retail stores, the salesperson interacts with many departmental leaders such as buyers, merchandisers, and general managers to ensure that aspects like merchandising, communication, product availability, and competitive performance are addressed profitably. Additionally, there may be a head office that will require a separate executive management operation.

In informal markets, the salesperson typically meets with the owner, or their employee as a one-man band responsible for all business agenda, including purchasing, merchandising, and general management.

So, there is need to adjust one's approach when dealing with the two separate retail types.

Selling Skills and Sales Preparation

To be successful as a salesperson, being prepared is essential. Sadly, this is rarely given enough attention. Before a salesperson goes to sell in the informal markets, there are some basic aspects of sales preparedness that they need to have:

Mental Preparation

The best salesperson in the informal market is the one who is prepared to face rejection ten times and still pick themselves up for another shot at success. They recognize the market they are dealing with and accept the ups as much as the downs. They understand that the work ahead will be tough, gruelling, dirty, and exhausting but at the end of the day rewarding. This means the salesperson must go into the market with tons of self-motivation, mental stamina and a strong drive to push through obstacles.

Routine distractions like home chores and family affairs must be methodically dealt with ideally the day before, or after the day's work and not during the hours of operating in the trade.

Diary management with a clearly defined route plan must a norm of operation and every salesperson must have a to- do list and make sure that it is completed.

Dress code

Salespersons serve as representatives of both the organization and its products. Accordingly, they should dress in a manner that is suitable for their specific assignment. Even within informal market settings, there are unwritten standards for decorum as well as considerations regarding health and safety. Exercising prudent judgment is recommended.

Avoid wearing clothing such as shorts, crop tops, see-through materials, or garments that expose sensitive areas of the body, as these may not align with the dress standards expected by clients. Avoid wearing branded clothes that are not aligned to what you are selling. Imagine selling Pepsi while wearing a Coca-Cola shirt. The choice of attire can potentially affect perceptions of both individuals and the organization they represent.

For health and safety considerations, it is advisable to avoid wearing high heels, slippers, Crocs, sandals, and hard fashion shoes in informal markets.

Using gum boots and a poncho can be useful during the rainy season, although they may not be practical to carry on hot and dry days.

Avoid carrying handbags or purses; strap-on pouches are more convenient and safer.

Iron your clothes ahead of time for a smart appearance. Avoid ironing on workday mornings to prevent stress if there is no electricity (most African countries tend to ration power).

Personal Hygiene

Always pay close attention to your personal hygiene and make an extra effort to look after this aspect well in advance of the day of going to market. In hot climates, body odour is a common challenge faced by every salesperson when they are out in the market and there are cases when this can become a sales distraction.

- Bath thoroughly before and after going to the market.

- Drink water throughout the day to stay hydrated.

- Shave the armpits for presentability and to avoid extreme body odour cases.

- Use roll-ons and anti-perspirants to deal with bad body odours.

- Use body sprays but avoid using them to directly mask the odour. It will not work.

Selling Sales tools

To be a successful corporate salesperson, it is important to have a checklist of the personal tools you need and to make sure that all the tools are available before the day starts. Knowing this may also help you to avoid carrying unnecessary tools for the visits and weigh yourself down. Some of the ideal tools to carry with you into the informal trade may include:

- An employee ID to deal with authorities and to identify yourself to the retailers.

- Wearing branded clothing in line with the product you are selling occasionally does help to sell the product. Avoid wearing t-shirts or clothes with other brands advertised or inappropriate dressing as this can be counterproductive to your selling. The downside of branded uniforms is that it can make the salesperson a target to thugs in informal markets, especially if the brand in question may be perceived as high value. I witnessed this when selling cigarettes that are considered cash-cows in informal markets.

- If the salesperson uses a bicycle or motorised vehicle, the asset must be checked daily using a checklist to ensure everything is available and functional. You need to avoid disrupting the selling day because of a breakdown that could have been avoided.

- I recommend that you always sell with a mobile reporting tool. The mobile device for reporting must have sufficient data, SMS and call bundles available for the day. The device should be fully charged and if possible, also carry a power bank to recharge midday if necessary.

- Always carry a small notebook and pen as well as any stationery for invoicing and receipting. This can be your backup plan if the mobile reporting device fails.

- The salesperson should always carry some posters or other merchandising display and giveaway material to leave with the retailers.

- It is essential to ensure that all products supplied to the retailer achieve full sell-through. Securing optimal visibility in a kiosk can be challenging, as consumers often view merchandise through a limited display window.

- It is important to announce your product with merchandising point of sale material displayed outside the store.

- The salesperson must always carry a filled-up water bottle for continuous rehydration. This is important given the nature of work where one walks in the open heat.

Product knowledge

All salespeople must be able to fully explain the product that they are selling, and they must at least have tasted (tested) or sampled the same products. It is amazing how many salespeople sell what they themselves have never tried.

- Have a physical price list, brochure or leaflet that explains the product.

- It helps for salespersons to carry a FAQ card with answers for frequently asked questions.

Pace yourself - Follow the Market Pattern

Understanding the trends in the market is critical for salespersons to enjoy success in their business. While the market trends may differ for a given product, understanding these patterns enables sales professionals to optimize their efforts, ensuring they are most effective during key selling periods, and schedule breaks during slower intervals.

- For instance, in the FMCG sector, peak sales typically occur between 6am and 10am, accounting for approximately 60% of daily sales. This is when most informal market traders also spend their daily available funds. Eighty percent of peak sales may be achieved by lunchtime.

- The remainder of their sales tend to take place after 2pm, with an additional surge from 5pm to 8pm especially in outlets offering food or alcohol products. Adhering strictly to a standard 8am–5pm schedule, as is common in office settings, is often not conducive to maximizing success within informal markets. Plan to visit the market when it is most effective.

Sharpen Your Communication and win the Market

In the hustle and bustle of market visits, there's often little time for preparation. But one thing you can never afford to overlook is communication. It is the heartbeat of every sale. And in the informal retail space, it is often the one skill that makes or breaks your deal.

- Clarity is Key: It is astonishing how many salespeople struggle to describe their product in 15 seconds. Some mumble through their pitch; others would not have even tried their own product! Your confidence and clarity begin with one simple rule: know your product inside out, understand its value, anticipate questions, and rehearse your pitch until it flows naturally.

- Adapt Your Personality to the Audience: If you are bold and outgoing—fantastic! But remember, not every customer responds to high energy. Effective communication means knowing when to dial it up... and when to dial it down. Tailor your delivery to the personality of the retailer you are facing. Assertiveness is impactful when used wisely.

- Speak Their Language. Respect Their Culture: Success in the field hinges on cultural intelligence. Speak the local languages used in the market and follow the customs of the area. A male salesperson meeting a veiled Muslim woman should avoid initiating physical contact. And if a retailer offers the same to a veiled salesperson, they should know how to decline gracefully while keeping the conversation warm and professional. Respect opens doors.

- Dress the Part. Prepare to Impress: Know your audience before you step out. Dress appropriately for the occasion and tailor your presentation to suit the local context. It is not just about looking professional, it is about being intentional, respectful, and relatable.

These are just a few silent drivers for successful selling. We shall go into more detail now, to home in on the core characteristics of those drivers that will give you maximized success in selling to the informal markets.

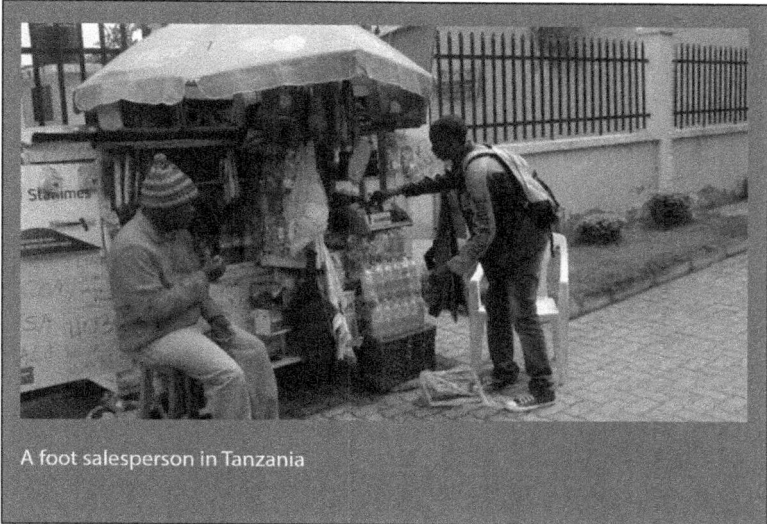

A foot salesperson in Tanzania

A bicycle salesperson in Nairobi

> **"** Just eight minutes can open a door to a lifetime customer. **"**

THE 8-MINUTE SELLING METHOD

Let us face it, attention spans are shrinking. The average human attention span, which was once fifteen seconds, is now just eight seconds. Technology has accelerated everything, and we are feeling it in how we talk, consume, and make decisions—especially in fast-moving business environments.

In formal investment pitches, you typically get three to five minutes to hook an investor. Just look at the popularity of shows like Shark Tank and Lions' Den—within minutes, you can spot whether a pitch will win or flop. The rest is just negotiation. But when selling in informal markets— particularly to small kiosk and tabletop retailers—you need a method that is fast, compelling, and proven.

The 8-Minute Selling Method

The 8-minute selling method

We created this method internally in our organisation to meet the demands of informal FMCG retail. It is a streamlined, step-by-step approach that fits the tight rhythms of sellers and buyers on the ground. From greeting to closing a sale, it walks the salesperson through the following:

- A confident and engaging introduction
- A concise but impactful explanation of your product or service
- Handling objections with clarity and empathy
- Closing the sale and persuading the retailer to buy

In selling to informal retail, you typically have fifteen to thirty seconds to spark interest. That is your entry point.

So, why eight minutes?

Because it works! Spending more than eight minutes risks interrupting the retailer's business —and it leads to diminishing sales returns. Efficiency matters in informal markets. Respect for the informal trader's time builds trust and this method is designed to gain you that trust, respect and success in selling.

Trained and Tested Across Africa

We used this method of selling to kiosks and tabletops across categories selling everything from snacks to soaps. We developed a simple selling process and rolled it out across East and Southern Africa working with over two thousand corporate salespeople. The results were phenomenal: there was a significant improvements in sales, increased volume sales conversions, stronger client relationships and faster transactions per salesperson.

This method can work with small supermarkets and modern trade but with modifications to the times to allow for visiting the different departments.

This is not just theory; it is a proven tool built for the streets, the stalls, and the retail sales moments that matter.

The 8-Minute Sales Call: A Winning Formula for Informal Markets

Step 1: Assess, Connect, and Greet with Intention (1 Minute)

As you arrive at the store, take a moment to assess the environment.

- Is the shop well stocked and tidy?

- Are customers browsing or buying?

- What is the retailer's energy like? Cheerful, stressed, or indifferent?

This quick scan will help you tailor your pitch effectively.

A fully stocked shelf with clean dusted products neatly presented reflects a healthy business. Conversely, a shop with empty shelves may reflect a cashflow challenge with the business. Understanding this quickly can determine the direction of your sales pitch.

Now, walk in with purpose to the store entrance. Remember, the retailer may be busy, and customers always come first. Never interrupt a customer interaction—instead, wait for them to finish their transaction and then make your move. Confidence with respect is key.

Your greeting sets the tone, so use the local language and a warm, culturally appropriate approach. In the post-

COVID era, go for a friendly nod or verbal greeting instead of a handshake unless physical contact is expected.

Important: Even if you are exhausted from a long day in the field, remember this is the retailer's first interaction with you today. Re-energise. Show up fresh. Smile. They are your most important client in that moment.

Quick Tip: Before stepping in, pause outside the shop. Breathe, focus, and adjust your tone and energy to the mood inside.

Step 2: Find Common Ground & Build Rapport (1 Min)

Connection creates conversion. Find a shared moment or observation that you can create a shared moment with the retailer:

- "I see you already stock our detergent—great placement!"
- "This weather is something, eh?"
- "Your display really stands out today."

Genuine compliments matter, especially in informal markets where recognition is rare. Keep it real. A small kind word can melt walls, especially if it is your first visit. Listen to their response and adjust accordingly. If the retailer responds warmly, continue. If they rush you or ask you to leave, respect that and close out professionally using Step 8. This keeps the door open for another time.

Step 3: Introduce Yourself and Set Intent (30 Sec.)

If it is a new visit and the vibe is good, introduce yourself, clearly stating your name, your company or brand that you are representing and the reason you are visiting (most times, it is to sell, but it could be to help with merchandising or to install point of sale material).

Whatever the case, keep this stage brief and upbeat. Do not dive into the detail yet because you need to see if the retailer is up for it.

Pro Tip: Rehearse this 30-second intro in front of a mirror. Refine your tone, speed, and expressions until they feel effortless and authentic. Be ready to adapt it based on the situation inside the shop.

Step 4: Show the Product, Do Not Just Talk (2 Mins)

Now that you have set the tone, proceed to showcase your product. The best way to engage a retailer is through experiential selling. Let them see, hold, and feel the product—even if it is just a sample. People buy what they experience. Just like you would not buy a phone without touching it, retailers want to "peruse" before purchasing. If you cannot carry everything, use smart tools like compact brochures or short, visual PDFs or clear, mobile-friendly videos using your tablets or phones. If you must use your smartphone or tablet, please ensure that it is well charged and the screen is clean!

Have at least one physical product in hand. When they touch it, it creates a psychological bond—and that makes it harder to hand it back without closing on a sale.

Step 5: Make a Targeted Offer (2 Minutes)

Before a salesperson begins their day, they must know what they want to achieve. This means setting a clear sales target and planning how to reach it. For example, if Grace wants to sell 500 sachets today, she must first decide how many shops she will visit and what types of shops they are. Tabletops, kiosks, and small supermarkets all have different buying power. Some will buy small quantities, while others can take more. By knowing the store types and how much each usually buys, Grace can break down her target into smaller goals for each visit.

She might plan to visit 18 shops in total. Tabletops may

buy $10 worth of stock, kiosks may buy $20, and small supermarkets may buy $50. If each sachet costs $0.50 and comes in packs of 12, Grace can calculate how many packs she needs to offer each shop to reach her goal. This helps her avoid guessing and makes her offer more realistic.

When Grace enters a shop, she should first look at the stock levels. If the shelf is low, she can suggest a refill. If the product moves fast in that area, she can recommend a larger restock. Her pitch should be based on what she sees, what she knows about the store's size, and how often that type of store sells out. This makes her offer feel helpful, not pushy.

If Grace uses a mobile app, it can show her the store's past orders, how often they reorder, and what products they prefer. This helps her make smarter decisions. She can use this data to suggest the right quantity and explain why it makes sense. She can also talk about the benefits of restocking now, like saving time, getting support in future visits, and keeping up with customer demand.

Setting targets per store is not just about numbers. It is about understanding the store's habits, knowing your product well, and using local knowledge to guide your pitch. When you do this, your offer becomes more than a sale—it becomes a solution. And when you bring solutions, you build trust, repeat business, and stronger results.

Step 6: Handle Objections (1.5 Minutes)

When you offer a product, the shopkeeper will usually respond in one of three ways. First, they may say yes, which means they are ready to buy. In that case, you should close the sale and, if possible, offer a little more to increase the order. Secondly, they may say, "maybe," which means they are unsure. In that case you will need to understand why and help them feel more confident.

Lastly, they may say, "No." Even then, you should stay respectful, listen carefully, and leave on good terms so you can return another day.

Objections are a normal part of selling and when they arise, it is important to handle them professionally. Below are a number of steps you can follow when faced with objections:

- First, listen carefully. Let the shopkeeper speak without interrupting them. Watch their body language. Are they crossing their arms, looking away, or hesitating? These signs help you understand how they are really feeling. Show that you are listening by nodding, keeping eye contact, and staying quiet until they finish. In African conversations, we can also acknowledge with "oohs" and "ahas", but be careful not to lengthen the conversation, antagonise the customer or embolden them incorrectly.

- Second, show empathy. Let them know you understand their concern and remember that profit is their highest priority. Say things like, "I understand why you feel that way," or "Others have shared that same worry." This helps the shopkeeper feel heard and respected.

- Third, ask questions to understand better. If they say the price is high, ask, "Is that compared to other brands or based on your budget?" If they say they do not have space, ask, "Is storage the main issue, or are you worried about how fast it will sell?" These questions help you find the real reason behind the objection.

- Fourth, adjust your offer. If you first offered a big pack, maybe now you offer a smaller one. If you talked about quantity, now talk about profit. Share stories of other shops that tried the product and saw good results. This builds trust and shows that your offer is practical.

- Fifth, check if your response helped. You can ask, "Does that sound better to you?" Or watch their body language. If they seem more relaxed or start asking questions, you are on the right track.

- Sixth, if they seem ready, close the sale. Say something like, "Shall we start with the 12-pack and see how it goes?" This makes it easy for them to say yes.

- Seventh, if they are still unsure, offer a smaller test. Say, "Would you be open to trying just one variant to see how it performs?" But do not push too hard. If they still say no, thank them kindly and move on. Being polite keeps the door open for future visits.

One powerful tool in selling is called mirroring and matching. This means you copy the shopkeeper's energy and style. If they are calm, you stay calm. If they are lively, you show energy too. This helps build a connection. People subconsciously trust those who behave in a familiar way. When you mirror their tone, pace, and posture, they feel more comfortable with you. It is a quiet way to build agreement without saying much.

Handling objections is not about winning and getting an order every time. It is about understanding the customers' requirements and meeting them in an ideal win-win scenario. When you listen, adjust, and stay respectful, you build trust. And in informal markets, remember that you shall visit the same stores and region several times more in future, so a "no" today could become a "yes" tomorrow.

Step 7: Close the Sale (2 Minutes)

Closing a sale is like finishing a race—you have done the hard work, now you need to finish strong. It should feel smooth, not rushed. A good close is never forced. It comes from being ready, staying calm, and knowing what to do next. When the shopkeeper agrees to buy, your job is to complete the transaction quickly and professionally.

Before you start, make sure the shopkeeper is clear on what they are buying and how much it will cost. Say the total amount out loud before printing the invoice. This helps avoid surprises. Sometimes, when the final invoice is printed, the shopkeeper may feel the amount is more than what they expected. That can cause delays or even cancellations. So always confirm the final bill first.

If you are carrying the product with you, then you can hand it over right away and collect payment. Then move to the invoicing stage. If the delivery will happen later, you can issue a proforma invoice and explain when the goods will arrive and who will bring them. Either way, make sure the process is clear and simple.

Use mobile apps or automated tools if you have them. They help you move fast and avoid mistakes. Do not waste time looking for invoice books or counting stock in front of the customer. That makes you look unprepared and can break the flow of the sale. The closing stage should take no more than two minutes.

Think of it like a football striker in front of the goal. The pressure is high, and the moment is big. But the best strikers stay calm; focus, and then score. The same goes for sales. When you feel that rush of excitement, do not let it make you clumsy. Practise your closing lines. Practise how to invoice. Practise how to deliver the product. Practise how to collect payment. Practise until it feels easy and natural.

Closing is not just about getting the money. It is about leaving the shopkeeper feeling good about the decision. When you close well, trust increases and they are more likely to buy again. Furthermore, they are more likely to recommend you. That is how you build strong relationships and long-term success.

Step 8: Log, Schedule, and Leave Right (30 Seconds)

The way you end your visit matters just as much as how you began. Before you leave the shop, always confirm the next time you will return. This shows the shopkeeper that you are serious, reliable, and respectful of their business. When you keep your word and come back as promised, you build trust. That trust is what keeps the door open for future sales.

In informal markets, traders often hold small amounts of stock. They sell quickly and need to restock often. That means your visits must be regular. Weekly or fortnightly visits are best. They help the shopkeeper keep their shelves full without putting pressure on their cashflows. After about six successful visits, you may reduce the frequency slightly, especially if the shop starts using mobile apps or online tools to reorder. But never let a month pass without checking in. If you do, you risk losing the relationship and the sales.

Even if you did not make a sale today, your visit still matters. Showing up consistently proves that you care. It shows that you are dependable. And it helps the shopkeeper remember your brand when they are ready to buy.

If you use a digital sales tool, update it immediately after the visit. Record what happened—whether it was a sale, a discussion, or just a check-in. This helps you track your progress and plan better. It also helps the next salesperson who may take over your route. Your update will enable them to see what you did, what worked, and what did not. That way, they do not repeat mistakes or miss important details.

Leaving right means leaving with respect, with a plan, and with a record. It is the final step in your selling method, and it sets the tone for your return. When you log, schedule, and exit properly, you build a rhythm of trust, service, and success.

Continuous Training on the 8-Minute Selling Steps

As a salesperson or an executive managing a team of salespeople who work in the informal markets, it is important to ensure that sufficient training is undertaken by the representatives. You can adopt any or all of the below methods of training to maximise the potential of your teams.

Workshops & Coaching

It is recommended that every salesperson attends training on a regular basis. This can be at the office with senior staff or at a workshop. Training routinely allows them to layer their skills gradually, starting with mindset, then conversation structure, then conversion techniques. It is also an opportunity for them to meet their peers and share ideas and adapt their mode of selling.

Role-Playing & Simulation

Practising sales scenarios with peers or coaches enables safe experimentation. They can rehearse how to respond to tough questions, present value propositions, or negotiate deals from formal office training. When adapted to culturally relevant contexts, role-playing becomes even more impactful.

Learning by Doing

Street-level selling teaches and equips beyond what can be read in textbooks. Encouraging salespeople to actively engage with diverse customer segments helps sharpen their instincts—whether it is navigating price objections or tailoring offers based on body language and buying cues. Allow the salespersons to go to market and get their feet dirty.

Digital Practice Tools

Develop apps as well as video and voice-recording

tools that can be used to rehearse sales scripts, track improvement, and analyse the delivery tone or pacing. Salespersons should spend as little time as possible visiting the office or doing administration, and so you should be able to send this information to them digitally and track their lessons using digital apps.

Mentorship & Peer Feedback

Pairing novice sellers with experienced ones builds community and accelerates learning. Shadow selling with the salespeople in the informal markets is effective for testing and sharing feedback after every customer interaction and experiencing stories from the field. This reinforces experiential knowledge.

A Final Thought on the 8-Minute Selling Process

Selling in informal markets is not just about making money. It is about building trust, showing respect, and creating strong relationships. Every visit you make is a chance to show your professionalism. Just like performers practise their lines or athletes train for their moves, you must practise your selling steps until they feel natural.

The more you rehearse, the more confident and prepared you become. Whether the sale goes through or not, each visit teaches you something. Learn from every result and keep improving.

In informal markets, traders work hard and make fast decisions. They deal with small stock levels, quick turnarounds, and tight cash flows. That means they value salespeople who are clear, respectful, and reliable. When you show up on time, speak with honesty, and offer real value, you earn their trust. That trust leads to repeat business, referrals, and long-term success.

Always pay attention to the mood of the area. Some places are busy and loud, others are quiet and slow. Match your energy to the environment. Speak in a way that feels familiar and friendly. Do not rush. Do not push. Connect with the trader as a person first, then as a customer. When you do that, your pitch becomes more than a sale—it becomes a conversation.

Respect is key. Respect their time, their space, and their decisions. Even if they say no today, leave with dignity. That way, they will welcome you back tomorrow. And when they are ready to buy, they will remember how you made them feel.

The 8-minute selling method is not just a routine. It is a mindset. It helps you stay focused, work efficiently, and professionally. It helps you bring your best to every shop, every time. And when you do that, you do not just sell— you grow – you grow your brand, your income, and your reputation.

4

SELLING ETIQUETTE &
BUSINESS HABITS

TIME MANAGEMENT: THE SILENT SUPERPOWER OF SELLING EXCELLENCE

Being late is not about time. It is about respect. That may sound dramatic. But let us test it.

Would you show up late to meet your Head of State?

Would you arrive less than an hour before take-off time for a flight that you paid for?

Would you stroll into your graduation ceremony after the door closing time?

Would you walk into a courtroom after the hearing time?

No? Then lateness is not about circumstances; it is about priorities. The truth is, tardiness is a choice, and it reflects how much value we place on the people, events, or opportunities in front of us.

"African Time" – A Continental Irony

Across the 15 plus African countries I have worked in, there is a shared inside joke among my colleagues that "nothing ever starts on time." For some events, 8:00 AM invitations mean 9:30 AM. Organisers sip their tea while early attendees wait to be served or offered access to the conference room. Speakers talk on and on beyond their allocated slot. By the end of the day, everything is delayed—except the meal breaks. As one colleague once put it, "In Africa, we reward latecomers and punish the punctual." Painful, but true.

The Punctual Person's Perspective

Do we ever consider what it takes to be on time? Waking up at dawn, skipping breakfast, maybe missing out on seeing off the kids to school and then dodging the traffic chaos. Then arriving fifteen minutes early and waiting patiently for doors to open. You have sacrificed family time and other potentially profitable work and probably received a police ticket for a traffic violation just to be on time for that meeting. Now imagine being asked to wait another 45 minutes—because "other people are still on their way."

That is not flexibility. That is disrespect disguised as culture.

Time is Money—literally, in Sales

In informal markets, time is everything. We will use our field rep Grace again here. Picture this: Grace is scheduled to visit twenty informal market shops in one day. If she successfully sells to ten of them at ten dollars each, that will be one hundred dollars that she expects to earn for the company in a day.

But then for some reason she leaves home late, citing power issues. By the time she got on the road, she found herself stuck in traffic. Because of this, she fails to visit six viable shops and only manages to make forty dollars out of the possible one hundred.

If she earns a 10% commission, she has lost six dollars' worth of incentive for the day. To the company, she has lost sixty dollars' worth of sales in a single day. Now multiply that across one hundred sales reps, and the company loses six thousand dollars in a single day. Let us not forget, she has also broken visit promises to six outlets that now do not consider her reliable, so the retailer will now place fresh orders with her competition, and your organisation may have lost at least four weeks of future business before you can regain the lost retail merchandising space.

Now that Grace has earned only four dollars instead of ten dollars in commission, she will become demoralised, citing low income. Consequently, she reduces her effort as she seeks "extra" income to supplement her monthly expenses – blaming the company for excessively tough targets. That spiral leads her to being tardier in her work delivery and ultimately results in disciplinary action or resignation.

That is the hidden cost of tardiness. It is not just bad manners; it is bad business.

How to Master Time (Even in an "African Time" World)

1. *Stop Excusing Lateness—Even for Traffic*

Everyone knows the rush hour times in their cities and the directions that are affected the most. If you are a salesperson, plan your travels so that they accommodate traffic. Leave early. Prepare for delays. If you are still running late, call your client ahead of the appointment time to advise them of the delay.

Speaking of lateness, we once worked with a corporate client generating fifty thousand dollars in monthly sales. They were typically pleasant to be around and very cooperative. On one occasion, we arrived late for a presentation due to traffic. The client took our tardiness and excuse as disrespect and brashly asked us to leave his premises and subsequently removed our products from their promotion in favour of a competitor's.

As a result, we lost a fifty-thousand-dollar promotional order. Following this incident, we banned anyone from citing traffic as a reason for lateness. And considerable effort was required to restore the business relationship with our client.

2. Use a Calendar—And Leave Room to Breathe

Do not cram your calendar with back-to-back meetings without making room for breaks. Plan for travel time, security checks (especially where the client is in a security area), unexpected delays and recovery time after intense meetings. Simply put:

> Overloaded calendars =
> under performance and burnout

One of our sales representatives kept on missing their store visit targets. It turned out that in our calculations for store visits, we had zero buffer time for the reps to recover from a sale, to have a quick regroup and rest. From that finding, we recommended that he and other supervisors add five-minute breaks after every store visit and thirty-minute breaks after every three hours of work. As a result, their closing rate improved by 35%, and their visit efficiency was above 95%. The overall income from the sale team increased by 25% with this simple fix.

3. Arrive Early—Not Just on Time

There's a golden rule that I always try to instil in my sales teams: "Early is on time. On time is late." I also had to learn this. What this means is that you should always strive to arrive fifteen minutes prior to any meeting. This should allow you to have adequate time to park calmly, clear security, compose yourself, hydrate, breathe and review your pitch.

I remember a certain visit I made to a difficult client. I was already five minutes late when I got to the premises. Then I had to climb four flights of stairs in a dusty building to meet the buyer. When I got to the top floor, I was panting and gasping for air. The receptionist immediately ushered me to the conference room.

The manager was waiting for me, and without exchanging some pleasantries, he went straight into the numbers, asking for discounts, demanding a return of stock, and throwing all sorts of numbers at me.

My instinct quickly kicked in. I knew that if I agreed to any numbers in my huffing and puffing state, I would make a big mistake. So, I stopped him in his tracks while pulling out my laptop. He then twisted the conversation and said, "You are not ready. Come back tomorrow," and left. It was not the first time this trader used this tactic of negotiating under pressure – but because I had noticed his tactic, I never got that second chance. That client was passed on to another salesperson the following week – on his request.

4. Plan Your "Perfect Day"

We sat with our field sales team and listed all the reasons they were late on any given day. It was an endless list. But from it, we co-created what we called a "Perfect Day Plan". From wake-up routines to bedtime, we detailed all the to-do's that a normal sales representative should take care of for their day to be wholly effective:

- The night before – do your preparation work like ironing and making meal packs for yourself and kids.

- In your morning routines, wake up on time and freshen up and eat as necessary. Do your family routines, and prepare kids for school. Leave home on time to avoid traffic jams.

- Daily hydration – almost all our sales representatives

complained of headaches, especially in the afternoons while working in the informal markets. Each rep got a bottle holder stitched onto their bag and was advised to drink at least one litre per day. Dehydration is a terrible sales killer.

- Every salesperson must, the night before, know the basics of the area they are to sell: the target stores they will visit and their target sales value. This mental preparation ensures that the salesperson goes to market clear of their objectives.

- In addition, each salesperson needs to be clear on each route plan and where and when they will take their breaks (five minutes after each store visit and thirty minutes after every three hours.)

Within two weeks of implementing the Perfect Day mode, the afternoon sales increased by 40%, and we had fewer complaints of fatigue, and staff retention improved.

5. Treat Every Meeting with Respect—Big or Small

Whether you are meeting a small kiosk owner or a boardroom executive, arrive on time, and end the meeting on time. Do not let someone else's late schedule ruin your schedule.

Still on meetings, we also realised that meetings do not necessarily need to be scheduled for a full hour. For some reason, every slot ended up being hourly, and we would naturally talk on and on to just exhaust the hour. When we changed our meetings to 15 minutes, they became more focused, pragmatic and less dreary.

One CEO I worked under had a strict rule: doors close exactly at the scheduled start time. If you were late—even by a minute—you would find the door closed and could neither knock nor open that door. You effectively missed the entire meeting.

Very harsh? Maybe. Effective? Absolutely. We were never late after missing the first meeting. Post-Covid, most meetings are now online, and we need to have the same level of diligence when it comes to timekeeping.

6. *If You Are Hosting an Event—Respect the Early Birds*

As we have already mentioned, please stop punishing those who arrive on time. If you must start later than the advertised time, then:

- Offer meaningful early bird activities and rewards— networking, entertainment, or photo booths.

- Start with smaller sessions that add value before the main event.

- Avoid wasting time with filler music or awkward chitchat. Read your clientele.

At one product launch, we offered early arrivals an exclusive Q&A with the guest speaker and author, who happened to be quite popular in the country. This privilege was not offered after the conference. Not only did it make the event feel premium, but more guests arrived before the official start time next time.

Conclusion: Timekeeping is not "Un-African"

We are not living in yesterday's Africa anymore. We are competing globally. Whether you are in Nairobi, Lagos, Kigali or Accra—time has economic value. Every minute lost is a lost opportunity, a delayed sale, or a damaged relationship. I hope that we can move past the joke of "African Time" and lead with discipline, respect, and efficiency. Because when you respect time, you command respect.

66

Good etiquette opens doors
that money cannot.

99

BUSINESS ETIQUETTE IN SELLING

Etiquette is not outdated; it is empowering. It reminds us how to honour others, how to command respect without demanding it, and how to build a legacy—not just a reputation. For those of you selling in the informal markets or dreaming of climbing the corporate ladder, these lessons, although few, seriously matter. In the chapters that follow, I will share the practical tools, the quiet truths, and the loud breakthroughs that helped our youth transform from hesitant interns to promising executives.

"The future is not just in your hustle; it is in your habits."

Sitting in a meeting

We used to host or attend a lot of meetings with suppliers and with retail customers. Many times, we would walk into a boardroom, and I would see my young team members casually taking the seat at the head of the table. They would slump in them, spread their literature on the table and make themselves comfortable. It took several warnings and lectures before some of them got it. Then they taught their colleagues, but every new team that came did not seem to get it.

It is important to know where to position yourself when you enter a meeting. In formal meetings, if a table is rectangular or oval, whether at home or in boardrooms, the ends of the table are for the leader of the meeting. Do not sit at the head unless you are the head for that moment. Do not fake sitting there as a joke. Do not excuse your action by saying, "That is where I am headed." If you are not directly invited to sit there, do not! Otherwise, one day you will be embarrassingly removed from that seat and, worse, end up compromising your effectiveness in that meeting.

What I am talking about is even supported by the Bible. Jesus gave an example of being invited for a wedding and allocating yourself a high seat. He exhorted the audience to sit in the lowest place so that when the host comes, they invite you to a higher seat. The reason for taking the low seat instead of the higher seat is for you not to be humiliated when someone much more senior arrives and you are asked to move. You do not want to be embarrassed.

Meeting etiquette

Annually, millions of young people complete tertiary education and enter the corporate world. Unfortunately, the colleges teach everything else but the basics of business etiquette. When you sell in informal markets or work in a corporate environment, meetings are an important aspect of that work.

To make sure we are all aligned, a meeting is when two or more people come together to discuss one or more topics. So, you are in a meeting when you sit with a retailer to sell them your product. You are in a meeting when you are talking to your supervisors and colleagues trying to map a way forward. You are in a meeting when you are sitting in a boardroom presenting to executives. Every interaction that you have that requires a decision is a meeting, and every meeting is an opportunity to present or be presented with a scenario and to walk away with a decision. But what is the etiquette for being in such meetings?

Food during meetings

Today, it is normal to bring water, juice and even snacks

into meetings if they are not already provided. However, the consumption of that food should not be a distraction to the meeting and its flow. The sight, sound and smell of the food should not affect the meeting.

A corporate meeting is not the time to open your lunchbox of fish stew because your health demands that you eat. The chewing of gum with the occasional pops, or rummaging through sweet wrappers or crisp packets, are all a big no. Basically, do not bring elements that will disrupt the flow of a meeting (sight, sound and smell). To be safe, do not bring food to meetings unless you agree to be meeting over lunch or tea. A bottle of water is the safest thing to bring to any meeting.

Contribute to meetings

When you are invited to a meeting, there must be a purpose for your presence. Therefore, it is expected that everyone in attendance must contribute their thoughts. You should contribute; otherwise, do not attend.

It is, however, important to keep track of the conversation and know when to contribute so that you remain relevant and positive to the agenda. Avoid being the office joker with a humorous quip for every situation or continuously regurgitating what has already been said. Listen attentively to the proceedings. Do not shut off and then expect a rewind of a previous statement.

Keep your meetings short

As mentioned already when we talked about African Time, it is important to keep meetings short. One way of doing that is to move away from the default of one-hour meetings where people end up just rambling on to just exhaust the hour. I was guilty of that, and someone had to pull me aside to share some wisdom. Since then I have been insisting that individual (2-person) meetings do not exceed 15 minutes and group meetings cannot be longer than 30 minutes or less. Although this is not a fixed rule, it has drastically opened my diary.

For meetings to be short, it is critical that attendees share any presentations in advance and that the participants read the material before the meeting. Although this is a noble idea, most people attending the meeting will not read the material beforehand and will try to fake it in the meeting. The "Amazon way" is really feasible, where you allow a few minutes to allow everyone to read the material during the meeting and then resume the meeting discussions. The important thing is to keep to the scheduled meeting time.

Another option is to have a timekeeper that reminds attendees when the meeting should end. In online meetings, it is common to see people with back-to-back meetings just leave when it is time. So, it is important to manage time so that crucial points are cleared within the set time.

Take notes

Always bring a notebook and a pen to meetings. Write down your own notes, listing the actions you should individually implement. Learn to write corporate minutes. Appreciate corporate governance at an early stage.

While technology has vastly improved the functionality of tablets, phones and laptops in minute taking, and now we have AI tools that take minutes for us, there is always a place for note taking with your notebook and pen. It sends a message that you are indeed listening attentively. Also, it works as a backup should that AI tool that you depend on so much fail to deliver.

Greet your elders

It is just African and polite to greet your elders first! It is an act of simple respect, and there is no loss suffered in the act. Whether at the workplace or at home, it is un-African for an older person to have to acknowledge and greet a younger person. And when you do the greeting, be intentional; stop what you are doing, establish eye contact or at least get their attention and be clear in your greeting. It is five seconds of your life that will earn you a mountain of respect. This simple but important culture unfortunately is getting lost amongst our youths, who now expect to be greeted or acknowledged simply because they got to the workplace first or they have the same position as the older colleague.

Of course, in the office, you do not need to be shaking hands with everyone to announce your arrival. That would be over the top and very distracting.

In informal markets, it is vital to have your greeting etiquette with you when you meet your customers and your suppliers. Informal markets do not operate on contracts and formal paperwork; they operate primarily on a principle of relationships and the sanctity of spoken promises with witnesses.

So, you must know the greeting protocols of the region you are operating in. Furthermore, you must know how to be formal and how to be social with the same reverence presented to those older or younger than you as well as those senior or junior in business rank. You must show respect to all.

If you are publicly rude to colleagues and employees, your reputation will quickly sink, and opportunities will equally diminish in the market once you are branded as "having an attitude". It will be a one-brush characterisation that you will carry for the entirety of your career and close many promotion opportunities.

Body posturing

There is a field of study dedicated to understanding body language and how mirroring and matching another person's posture can influence negotiations. Even with thorough preparation and appropriate attire, nonverbal cues such as posture or repetitive gestures can affect the outcome of a meeting. For instance, habits like smoking or clicking a pen when nervous may be used against you by astute negotiators.

Your body language often communicates more in negotiations than your words. Sitting upright or leaning forward signals firmness, while poor posture can undermine what you say. As a result, even a strong presentation might not yield results if your nonverbal cues are inconsistent.

Watch your character at events

If you attend a corporate event and the DJ plays your favourite song, remember your place. It is not time to demonstrate your best moves if you wish to retain your job or reputation. Reserve those moves for your own private occasions and friends.

The abundance of alcoholic beverages at a meeting or event is not an invitation for you to overindulge and huddle as the drink boys, to taste every concoction you had never sampled before. If you are at an office event that has alcohol, it usually means the business wishes you to loosen up, network without the office rigour and connect with your associates and potential partners. It is not a licence to drink like a fish, get drunk and cause a scene.

If you are introverted and find interacting with people that you are not familiar with incredibly challenging, avoid hiding in a corner and, worse still, congregating with fellow fearful colleagues to observe and comment on the event.

To progress in your career, you must learn to stand straight, have some pre-planned conversation points and interact with a few people, including the top leadership.

I would suggest that you always have at least five starter conversation points. Below are some examples:

- *Ask a question that demands their insight:* "I came across a recent trend in the market that seems to be reshaping how we should approach selling. I am curious to know how this is playing out from your vantage point." This works well to signal intellectual curiosity and positions you as someone that consciously tracks macro and micro shifts in business.

- *Ask a purpose-driven question:* "I have been working with my team and exploring some new selling methods that avoid wholesalers. How did you tackle emerging market wholesalers in the past?" Leaders love talking about how they guided the past, especially if it is framed in terms of impact and transformation.

- *Ask a question that challenges:* "From your experience, what is been the most complex leadership issue you have had to navigate in the past year?" This approach invites reflection and subtly shifts the conversation toward meaningful dialogue—not just small talk.

- *Ask a question that makes them think:* "How do you ensure your team carries forward the values you have built into the organisation?" This opens the door to rich discussions on legacy, culture, and generational leadership.

- *Ask a question that exchanges perspective:* "I'm working on an initiative focused on [brief 1-minute concept]. I would love to hear your perspective and if it aligns with our goals." This one positions you as proactive and value-orientated, without overstepping. It lets leaders opt in for a deeper exchange.

Extroverts, on the other hand, may still use the above openers, but they would need to restrain themselves to avoid talking over others and not take over the conversation.

Mobile phone etiquette

I entered the working world before mobile phones existed, and all we had were landline phones, memos and fax machines as our primary communication technology. Yes, that was long ago, and it is hard to imagine that such a time existed. Mobile phones are now ubiquitous and have become an important part of our lives. Sadly, they have at times become unwelcome partners in the corporate world.

When meeting clients, customers, and suppliers, I encourage my team members to put away the phones (ideally place them in the purse or pocket) while on silent mode. Placing the phone on the table will only cause you to take regular peeks and demonstrate that the people you are meeting are not the most important at the time. Ignore the phone completely for the duration of the meeting – you can always return the call or answer the messages. You will not miss much that you cannot respond to after the meeting.

Give your phone to a secretary or assistant if you really cannot avoid missing a call. Of course, there is an exception for those that work for security services or critical services. In that case their operational manual is different from ours as salespeople.

Today's sales personnel use their mobile phones as their primary reporting tool. Now this brings about a conundrum. Do you bring out your phone while you are in a meeting to immediately report on your app? Can you take out your device to record minutes using AI apps? Maybe.

However, to date, I have not seen any salesperson that successfully gives full attention to a client while inputting reporting on their device. The solution I have always recommended is that you put away your device, write notes on a notepad, and then immediately after the meeting, input the results in your device before you go to the next appointment and while you are still within the geofence zone.

Alternatively, where necessary, have a dedicated person that will be taking notes while you, the key player, negotiate with the client. It is, however, important to note that due to costs there are a few companies nowadays that can afford to have a dedicated minute taker who is not contributing to the meeting!

Taking selfies and social media pictures while in a meeting is an absolute no. Even if it is a working lunch, save the Instagram moments for when you are on personal social time.

Certain apps like Whats App have become part of our corporate communication ecosystem. If you are in a corporate group, avoid abbreviating messages unless it is a given corporate term. This is crucial in groups that have mixed generations and age groups. Abbreviations, short-form conversations and social lingo should just be replaced with complete words and punctuation. Use AI to rephrase your statements if you are struggling. Not everyone in a corporate group will be within your clique and age bracket, and they may not understand or will not appreciate the gestures – unless the abbreviations are part of internal corporate jargon.

Limit being the office joker, forwarding numerous jokes and anecdotes. Even though it certainly helps to loosen the teams and the group, beware that it may become your career death knell when your performance is under question. Keep all that for your friends and family groups.

Dining etiquette

Be flexible. Any progressive salesperson must be able to adapt, blending seamlessly with the clients in the informal markets and sitting with a key retailer in a quality restaurant. Practise using all the cutlery on a standard dinner table in all environments. It is not snobbish to know when and how to use the different forks, knives, spoons and chopsticks on the table.

Just as it should be perfectly normal to dine with your hands at a local corner informal restaurant. You should be at home enjoying a three-course meal at a five-star hotel, as you should be comfortable in an informal restaurant.

If you go to a corporate meeting where formal dining is involved, taking a photo of the food or taking selfies or Snapchatting during the meeting is a big no. Focus on the agenda of the meeting and focus on your attendees. If your guests are doing it, that does not give you the grounds to do the same. Set and maintain a standard of professionalism, and the people that make the money-making decisions will notice.

Personal etiquette

Selling and operating in African informal markets can really bring out a contradiction of situations about personal etiquette. While trading in informal markets may seem like dusty and grimy work, requiring you to blend in with the community, it does not mean you should equally wear flip-flops and torn, filthy attire. The product you sell needs to be represented, and the customer (the trader) and the consumer must see you as an inspiration – the first representation of that product. So, dress appropriately.

Always know the dress code required for the informal market, any office, meeting or event. If you are not sure, ask. Most events these days specify the dress code. And if they do specify, please follow their guidelines. I would recommend a simple rule, "Dress right or dress up." This means, at least, dressing to the minimum standards required for the market, the office or the event, but if you are in doubt, dress beyond their requirement. It is better to go somewhere in a full suit and then remove the tie and jacket than to go in shorts to a semi-formal meeting.

You cannot be helped then.

While you may never have been reprimanded for any of the etiquette faux pas in the past, it does not mean that you did not cause any offence or that your actions did not impact your career. It was just ignored. Avoid at all costs anything with the potential of causing public embarrassment through an open rebuke, reprimand or negative gesture. Practise etiquette daily, and you will thank yourself later in life.

5

THE FUTURE
OF INFORMAL MARKETS

THE CASE FOR DIGITAL UNIFICATION

Africa's Trillion-Dollar Informal Retail Opportunity

Africa's informal markets are not remnants of a bygone era. They are living, breathing systems that continue to define how trade happens across the continent. Every day, millions of small outlets (kiosks, tabletops, salons, agro-vet shops, small supermarkets, food stalls, and hawkers) sustain the flow of goods and services to more than a billion people.

These markets may appear fragmented, but they are not failing. They are resilient, adaptive, and quietly massive in scale. Their decentralised nature, cash-based trade, and human connections form the very foundation of Africa's retail economy. The time has come to view them not as scattered pockets of trade but as one giant, unified marketplace. An untapped trillion-dollar opportunity.

The Scale of the Informal Market

Africa's population in 2025 is estimated at 1.46 billion people, spread across roughly 210 million households, assuming an average household size of seven. Using our established working ratio of one retail outlet for every ten households, this gives a conservative estimate of 21 million informal retail outlets across the continent.

Now consider this: if each of these outlets trades an average of US$50 per week, then the collective weekly turnover of the informal retail economy would amount to US$1.05 billion per week. Multiplied across 52 weeks, this equates to approximately US$54.6 billion annually in direct, small-scale trade transactions.

However, this figure represents only the retail layer. When we factor in the extended multiplier effect, that is, the stock replenishment from wholesalers, supplier distribution, transport, packaging, and associated services, then the full retail ecosystem easily scales into hundreds of billions of dollars in annual transactional value.

Even at this conservative baseline, Africa's informal retail economy is larger than the GDP of many individual nations. It is the heartbeat of African commerce, yet it remains largely unmapped, unmeasured, and ununified.

The Multiplicity of Africa's Informal Markets

Africa's informal market is not a single uniform entity. It is a complex network of overlapping market types that coexist and evolve within one another. In every city and rural centre, there are multiple layers of trade operating simultaneously:

At one end are hawkers and tabletop vendors, the entry-level entrepreneurs serving commuters and walk-by consumers. Next are kiosks and small supermarkets, providing consistent access to fast-moving consumer goods within neighbourhoods. Beyond these are more formal supermarkets, where variety and convenience meet aspiration. Parallel to this are specialised markets like salons, agro-vet stores, tailors, electronics dealers, and open-air marketplaces that operate as community trade anchors.

Each of these levels interacts dynamically with wholesalers, distributors, transporters, and micro-financiers. What appears informal is, in fact, an intricate value chain, self-organised through trust, frequency, and community relationships rather than formal systems.

This multiplicity is Africa's hidden strength. It ensures that no single disruption can break the supply of goods. It allows for deep market penetration where formal retail cannot reach. And it creates millions of sustainable income opportunities for youth and families, fuelling both resilience and social stability.

Why Informal Markets Will Remain Dominant

Despite the visible growth of shopping malls and chain supermarkets, the informal market will remain at least 80-90% of Africa's retail landscape for the foreseeable future. Several economic and cultural realities ensure this outcome:

1. Population Growth and Urban Density. Africa's urbanisation is outpacing formal retail infrastructure. Informal trade grows faster because it requires minimal setup cost and immediate community presence.

2. Cash-Based Economies. With limited access to credit and digital payments in rural and peri-urban areas, cash transactions remain king. Informal markets are the natural home of cash (liquidity).

3. Cultural Familiarity and Trust. Consumers buy where they are known, respected, and understood. Informal traders offer personalised service, flexible quantities, and emotional connection that formal retail cannot replicate.

4. Economic Flexibility. Informal traders adjust pricing and stock to daily realities. They can downsize, relocate, or reinvent faster than any modern retailer.

Even with the growth of e-commerce and formal retail structures, Africa's informal market is not shrinking; it is evolving. It is digitising, not disappearing.

The Power of Unification

If Africa's 21 million retail outlets were digitally unified into one interconnected marketplace, a continental supermarket of sorts, the implications would be transformative.

A unified digital retail ecosystem would mean that every outlet, from a small kiosk in Accra to a mini mart in Mombasa, could be visible, measurable, and connected to suppliers, financiers, and consumers. Real-time data would inform production, logistics, and policy decisions. Suppliers would no longer guess where demand lies.

Governments would collect fair taxes without punishing small traders. Banks could lend confidently using verified transaction data, and the requirement for collateral would be nullified.

For corporations, this level of visibility would unlock predictable distribution, efficient replenishment, a lower last-mile distribution cost and measurable growth.

For investors, it would create a structured, high-yield investment channel in what is currently the most under-monetised retail network on earth. For traders, it would open access to credit, training, and improved profitability.

In essence, unifying Africa's informal markets digitally would transform a fragmented economy into a continent-sized, data-driven supermarket, built on trust, technology, and inclusion.

A Call to Investors and Policymakers

The informal economy of Africa represents the largest remaining frontier for organised retail investment in the world. It already commands over 80% of all retail trade, employs more than 85% of Africa's workforce, and touches nearly every household on the continent daily. Yet it remains largely invisible to institutional finance, formal regulation, and multinational strategy.

The investor who builds or supports Africa's digital backbone for informal trade, a platform that integrates mapping, payments, logistics, and analytics, will not merely participate in the market but define it!

Such an initiative would not only yield strong financial returns but also deliver measurable social and economic impact: job creation, financial inclusion, food security, and the stabilisation of supply chains that serve more than a billion people.

This is not speculative. The technology already exists. The youth are digitally literate. The consumers are active. What is missing is the courage and capital to unify what already works.

Africa's informal retail economy is a trillion-dollar opportunity disguised as disorganisation. It does not need replacement; it needs recognition, coordination, and intelligent investment.

The Future Is Informal, and It Is Digital

The next retail revolution in Africa will not take place in shopping malls or luxury plazas. It will happen in the bustling corridors of informal markets, powered by data, logistics, and youth-led innovation. The continent's informal markets are not a problem to be solved; they are a system to be understood, scaled, and digitised.

The transformation of these markets into one unified digital ecosystem is no longer an idea for tomorrow. It is the opportunity of today. For those bold enough to see it, Africa's informal market is not a story of chaos; it is a story of scale.

Africa is moving. The market is alive. The only question that remains is:

Will you move with it?

PARTNER WITH INHERITEGE COACHES

The insights in this book are designed to give you practical tools, but the greatest impact is achieved when the tools are applied with guidance, accountability, and strategies tailored to your unique context.

Whether you are building your small hustle, expanding a corporate footprint into Africa's dynamic trade networks, hosting a regional event, or equipping students and professionals with practical sales and leadership skills, our team and our programs are designed to support you achieve lasting success and growth.

Inheritege Coaches, a division of BTL Consulting Ltd, exists to walk with individuals, corporate organisations and institutions through that journey.

Our focus is on measurable sales performance, market automation and expansion, leadership development and building legacies that empower communities as well as businesses.

To contact us, send an email to coach@inheritege.com or visit www.inheritege.com. Alternatively, simply scan the QR code below to connect with us.

Inheritege Coaches

www.ingramcontent.com/pod-product-compliance
Lightning Source LLC
Chambersburg PA
CBHW060526210326
41521CB00023B/2371